MILDEW, MUDPIES, AND MIRACLES

Mildew, Mudpies,
and Miracles

Gleeful Glimpses into the Whirl of a Woman's World

BERNADETTE McCARVER SNYDER

CHARIS

Servant Publications
Ann Arbor, Michigan

Charis Books is an imprint of Servant Publications especially designed to serve Catholic readers.

Published by Servant Publications
P.O. Box 8617
Ann Arbor, Michigan 48107

95 96 97 98 99 10 9 8 7 6 5 4 3 2 1

Printed in the United States of America
ISBN 0-89283-912-0

Library of Congress Cataloging-In-Publication Data

Snyder, Bernadette McCarver.
    Mildew, mudpies, and miracles : gleeful glimpses into the whirl of a woman's world / Bernadette McCarver Snyder.
        p.   cm.
    ISBN 0-89283-912-0
    1. Women—Prayer—books and devotions—English.   2. Christian life—Anecdotes.   3. Snyder, Bernadette McCarver.   I. Title.
BV4527.S635   1995
242'.643—dc20   95-31431
                                                                                                    CIP

Dedication

For all the wise and wonderful women
who have touched my life gently—
my mother, my sister, my teachers, my friends.
They have shown me how to look at the world
and see apple pandowdy instead of crab apples.
They have shown me that,
even in the midst of mud and mildew,
a woman can find miracles.

Contents

Introduction

Are you near the end of your rope and fresh out of cope? Is your life like a sweater with little fuzzies all over it? When you try to make it better by pulling a loose thread, does the whole thing start to unravel? I know how you feel.

As you thumb through this book, you will read all about my fuzzies and loose threads. You will also notice that this book wanders—just like my mind. Words written at the end of a rope do not always fall in sequence. That's why you might read about my son as a teenager in one chapter and as a toddler in the next or about my Halloween howls on a page AFTER my Christmas capers. But then you probably expected something like that to happen in a book about the whirl of a woman's world.

The famous author, Edith Wharton, once wrote, "I have sometimes thought that a woman's nature is like a great house full of rooms: there is the hall, through which everyone passes going in and out; the drawing room, where one receives formal visits; the sitting room, where members of the family come and go as they wish; but beyond that, far beyond, are other rooms, the handles of whose doors perhaps are never turned...."

As you "turn the handles" in this book, I hope you will find some smiles, some joy, some fun. You might also find, behind the doors, mudpies, mildew—or miracles.

1 A Touch of Magic

When I was a little kid, there was a "magic place" in my grandma's backyard. It was just a little shady spot between the foundation of the house and a large overhanging flowery bush—just big enough for a small person to crawl into and be hidden from the outside world. I used to go there—sometimes alone, sometimes with a playmate—and in that "secret garden," I could travel to exotic far-flung places, to lands of adventure and discovery, intrigue and excitement. And it didn't take money or advance scheduling. All it took was imagination.

When I grew up and got lost in the world of work and worry, I almost forgot the magic of withdrawing to a quiet place to dream, to plan, to drink in the beauty of the moment, to pray, and to just "be." But then my son came along.

Although he was busily into everything and usually kept me chasing after him, there would be times when I would look out my kitchen window and see him in the backyard—in his little log-cabin playhouse, arms crossed on the window sill, just staring off into space. Other times, I would see him, all alone, lying flat on his back in the grass, gazing at the clouds, totally oblivious to all around him. And I knew he was journeying into imagination as I had done so many years before. I knew he had found the magic.

Dear Lord, since then I've tried to hang onto the "secret garden" my son helped me recapture. When I get caught in the quicksand, I remind myself to reach out for that flowered branch that can pull me into a journey of dreams or back to the safety of quiet prayer and meditation and peace. I am so grateful, Lord, that you gave me this magic gift of imagination. How sad that some of today's children—and adults—are always hurrying to pre-scheduled games, club meetings, and activities, or sitting in

11

front of a TV screen, watching the results of someone ELSE'S imagination. Help us, Lord. Don't let us lose the magic.

2   My Cat—the Cook!

S omeone once told me that "observation" is one of the best ways to learn something. If that's true, my cat should be a great cook!

He watches every move I make whenever I'm in the kitchen. While I slice, stir, measure, or mix, his eyes never leave my hands. He's always hoping I'll drop something delicious and that he can beat me to it!

Sometimes, when I get tired of Big Brother Cat watching me so closely, I will do something really mean. I'll hold out a piece of whatever I've been chopping. My kittycat gets all excited and races over to take a sniff—only to discover I'm offering him an ONION.

You should see the look of disgust he gives me over his shoulder as he prances away with his nose in the air! Even after I've teased him with other goodies that he considers obnoxious like green pepper, green beans, and green cucumber—his hope remains green and fresh. He never gets discouraged. Every time I hold out a morsel, he hurries over, just in case I might have finally decided to offer something sensible—like liver or steak.

No matter how many times I fail him, he never gives up. No matter how many times he gets disappointed, he keeps hoping for better. This mellow yellow fellow may not have a very high I.Q. or a big bank account or even a "good" family background, but he knows more than most about persistence—and forgiveness!

..*.*.*

Dear Lord, help me to be as hopeful and as forgiving as my cat! No matter how dark the night or green the onion, help me to have enough faith and confidence to try one more time. Who knows? Maybe the next time might turn out to be the opportunity I've been waiting for—the brass ring, the pot of gold, the bed of roses, the steak to go with the onion. And even if it isn't, remind me to enjoy the reaching, the expectation, the journey.

Whether my ticket's stamped tourist or first class, you will be with me and that's reason enough for me to travel hopefully and happily, to make the most of every minute and put a smile into every mile.

3   We've Been Branded!

My son has led me astray—again. A spoonful at a time! Our house has been "rated X" because I usually BUY Brand X—or whatever is on sale at the supermarket each week. So for years, our freezer has known nothing but Brand X ice cream.

But one day, the son and heir had to go and eat at somebody else's house—somebody who could afford name-brand ice cream. Not just any name brand either, but the most expensive kind—the kind with no artificial ingredients, no artificial preservatives, and no half-price sales.

He came home and announced that he never wanted Brand X to pass his lips again. He had tasted the forbidden fruit and wanted more. I explained that my Brand X budget could not afford his newly acquired taste. He countered, saying he would promise to eat only half as much ice cream if I would promise to buy the expensive kind—and that would balance the budget. This sounded logical, and I've never been able to deal with logic, so I agreed.

I started buying him the "good" ice cream which he dutifully rationed out while his father and I pigged out on the generic kind of frozen calories. But one day, in a fit of wild abandon, I tasted the expensive brand.

And I liked it.

Soon I was sneaking a spoonful here, a bowlful there. And now Brand X didn't taste so good any more. I wanted the good stuff. Then my husband caught me indulging one day and asked for a taste. Now he too has been corrupted. Our house has gone from Brand X to X-pensive. And our budget is X-hausted.

*****

Dear Lord, it's so easy today to get spoiled, to become accustomed to little luxuries and decide Brand X isn't good enough any more. Yes, Lord, I know I don't have to feel guilty about an occasional luxury. There's nothing wrong in being satisfied to have half as much of something expensive rather than twice as much of something cheap. Just help me to be grateful for whatever I have, Lord, even when the budget says it has to be Brand X. And thank you, Lord, for giving me so many X-tra helpings of joy and wonder and happy X-pectations!

4 Finding the Fountain of Youth

Next Sunday, I think I'll wear my bathing cap to church! Actually, I guess I should call it a "swim cap" instead of a "bathing cap," since I never wear it to take a bath—although I might start doing that in the future. In fact, I may start wearing that swim cap wherever I go!

You see, today I was lucky enough to go swimming in an indoor pool in the middle of winter. That was wonderful, but I knew it would be a bit chillier than in the summer and I am one of those people who is only warm enough when the temperature hits "stifling." So I decided I would unearth my old swim cap and wear that to keep my head warm.

After a few minutes of my determined but amateurish crash-splashing, duck-paddling, and side-swiping sidestrokes, I warmed up enough to enjoy the refreshing exercise. But later, in the dressing room, as I was trying to stuff my damp body into dry clothes, I noticed that my head was the only area that was comfortably warm.

And since swim caps never keep my hair totally dry, I knew that the minute I took off the cap, my wet hair would set off a freeze alert and send my body into the sneeze-sniffle pattern. So I decided to drive home wearing the swim cap.

The pool is just a few blocks from my house and I knew that as soon as I got home, I could stick my wet head under a warm hair dryer. But as I was driving along, getting double-takes from every car I passed, I happened to glance in the visor mirror.

I was amazed to see that the cap had wrought a miracle!

True, I looked weird—but I also looked wrinkle-free. The cap fit so tightly, it had pulled all the wrinkles off my face! I guess it worked just like those expensive facelifts where the doctor takes "tucks" at your temples to empty the bags under your eyes.

Well, of course as soon as I took off my cap, the wrinkles returned. And it became obvious that the only way I could make time stand still would be to wear this swim cap wherever I go.

Maybe if I add a flower or a feather, people will think rubber hats are "in" and soon you'll be seeing wrinkle-free women in swim caps everywhere.

₊₊*₊*₊*

Dear Lord, isn't it strange how we have all gotten to the point where we will go to any lengths to look young—even if we also look ridiculous? We think young is best, young is beautiful, young is where the action is, young is irresistible. Actually, young is fleeting and irretrievable.

When I was young, old was beautiful and revered and honored. But, as usual, my timing was bad and I started getting "mature" just as "old" was OUT! Oh well, why should I worry? At least, Lord, YOU still love old as much as young. Thank you for loving me as I am... with or without a swim cap.

5   Watch Out!

Time stood still this week. My watch broke. Actually, it wasn't even the watch—just the watchband. But I soon found out that a watch on the wrist is worth two in the pocket.

Since I never knew what time it was, I didn't know if I was running early or late. It was late. I didn't know if I had more time than I thought to finish something or less time. It was less. I didn't know if I should hurry or take my time. I should have hurried.

I found out that, even without a watch to alert you, time marches on. One day I sat and chatted with a friend over coffee because I was sure I had plenty of time left to get my shopping done. I didn't. I drove serenely through traffic instead of fuming and fussing every time a driver got in my way because I was sure I had time to get to an appointment. I was wrong.

But all week, I had this euphoric feeling that I needn't hurry or scurry or even worry. Without a watch to warn me, I had no idea that I was running a day late and a dollar short all week. But you know what? By the end of the week, somehow everything got done anyway!

Maybe I just won't get that watchband fixed after all. It was a lot nicer to give my friend my undivided attention as I listened to her woes. I could empathize and sympathize better when I wasn't always glancing at my watch, wishing she'd talk a little faster.

It was a lot nicer not to be honking my horn and darting dirty looks at other drivers. It was a lot nicer to keep on an even keel instead of pushing my blood pressure to its boiling point, worrying about every minute wasted.

I'm always thinking or saying, "I just don't have enough time." But I do. I have all the time there is. I have from sunrise to sunrise, summer, winter, fall, and spring! Time is not on my hands—but it is IN my hands.

..*.*.*.*

Dear Lord, why is it that I can manage to get up earlier in the morning to get to an appointment, but not to spend time reading the Bible? Why is it I can somehow find time to get to the new movie I really want to see but can't always make it to evening church services? Why is it I can always find a little extra time to go to a party, watch a favorite TV show, or even read a book-of-the-month, but can't find extra time for prayer?

Forgive me, Lord. You gave me this insatiable interest in everything and everybody so I know you understand. I promise to find more time for quiet prayer and private time with you. But Lord, you and I both know that even when there is no quiet time, you are still always with me—at the party, the picnic, the movie, the mall. And don't we have fun, Lord?

6   Here's Mud in Your Pie

Pies just like Mom used to make—peach, apple, cherry, and MUD.

Yes, the most popular pies at our house were mud. My son had a love-at-first-sight relationship with mud. He saw it, he jumped into it, he bonded with it. And then I made the mistake of showing him how to make mud pies.

Actually, I probably didn't have to show him. He would have learned on his own. He and his mud stuck together as tightly as the discount sticker on that item you'd planned to give as a gift. And pies were not his only specialty. There was bucket-o'-mud, mug-o'-mud, and face-o'-mud.

Instead of a back yard sandbox, we had a mud hole. He and his friends spent many happy hours there, creating mud monsters, mud mountains, and mud to clog mother's washing machine. Some houses have mud rooms. Ours had a mud garage. If my son had had his way, we would have had a house-o'-mud!

･･*･*

Dear Lord, thank you for mud and memories. Without mud, how could we have flowers, grassy lawns, or photo albums with pictures of a little boy whose sparkly eyes and happy, gap-toothed grin shines out of that muddy face? Help parents to remember, Lord, that the kind of dirt that washes out is not so bad for children. It's the kind of dirt that gets dished out all too freely today on TV and rock videos, in movies and magazines, that can cause permanent damage and soil an attitude and a life forever.

Help us to recognize that kind of dirt before it gets "ground in" and accepted as a part of everyday life. May we avoid mud pies of the mind and tolerate only YOUR kind of mud—the kind that makes good gardens grow, the kind that is dug up by happy little boys and girls in backyard mudpuddles.

7   Gutter Muttering

I've been in the gutter again! The rains came, the gutter overflowed, and no one was home but me.

Because all those raindrops couldn't fit into our clogged gutter, they splashed over into a pool on the ground. Then, instead of staying there like good little raindrops, waiting their turn to soak into the lawn, they had to go adventuring.

They must have been very determined because they wandered around until they managed to find one tiny little crack in the foundation of our house and seep their way into the basement. I don't know how those raindrops got in there but I had a terrible time getting the damp things out!

I mopped. I wiped. I fumed. I fussed. I turned my hair dryer loose on the wet carpet and it blew its little motor out but the rug remained soggy and saggy. Finally, when I had dried up everything as much as possible, I surfaced and returned to the upper part of the house. My spirits remained in the downer part.

By now, the rain had stopped and I should have grabbed that chance to get out the ladder and climb up to unclog the gutter. Instead, I grabbed a cup of coffee and the opportunity to sit down and feel sorry for myself. That's when the rain started again, the gutter overflowed again—and so did my tear ducts.

* * * * *

Dear Lord, have you noticed how much better I am at crying than hying? If I had hied and hastened to unclog that gutter when I had the chance, I could have avoided the FIRST cleanup. Why do I spend so much time worrying about, and feeling guilty about, all the things I could and should be doing—instead of just doing them? Please help me remember how good it feels when a hard job is finally finished, off the chore list, and on the "done" list.

Help me to clean out my clogged gutter of "later, some day, soon" and get into the free-flowing spirit of "NOW! THIS IS THE DAY THE LORD HAS MADE." Let me rejoice and be glad and get my get-up-and-go unclogged.

8   No More Empty Pockets

It must be wonderful to be famous, or a genius, or handy with a hammer. Today I heard a story about an artist who was all three—and it gave me a great new decorating idea! It seems that this famous, handy genius decided to build himself a get-away work room.

Just as he finished, he realized he had forgotten to include a shelf where he could keep refreshments for those long get-away hours with the paint pots. Being an inventive sort, he grabbed up an old pair of many-pocketed coveralls from the floor and plastered them into a wall, pocket-side out. When the plaster dried, he had a handy spot for a thermos of coffee, iced tea, or genius-ade. He could even stock his pockets with snacks and stay in his get-away all day!

Now why didn't I think of that?

There are several pairs of my son's old jeans I would like to plaster into a wall or stuff into the garbage can or bury in the backyard. Of course, I don't have a get-away room, and practically every room is a work room, so it would be hard to decide which room would look best decorated with the pockets of plastered pants.

So as I stoop and scrub, droop and dust I guess I'll just meditate on the words of another famous person, Friedrich Wilhelm Nietzsche, who once said:

> When one has much to put into them,
> a day has a hundred pockets.

Dear Lord, I have much to put into a day: washing dishes, cooking, running errands, reading, writing, giggling, singing, talking to a friend, listening to a child, feeling your nearness. Those may not be the kinds of things Nietzsche had in mind, Lord, but I'm grateful for them all. Thank you for giving me such full days. My pockets may not have much money in them but they are FULL of blessings.

9 Is There a Gift Horse in the House?

If my husband had lived in ancient Rome, he might have gotten crowned.

According to history books, the Romans honored winners of their games and contests by crowning them with laurel wreaths. And I've often thought that in a contest to see which husband gave his wife the most unusual Christmas gifts, my husband would for sure be awarded the holly wreath (and I'd be glad to do the crowning.)

Actually, I should be getting accustomed to the presence of strange presents. He once gave me an autoharp in spite of the fact that I don't know how to play or even read music. He gave me a sewing box in spite of the fact that I don't sew. And he gave me a glamorous long rhinestone necklace that should only be worn with a slinky black evening gown. The only evening gown I own is red plaid flannel with a little white lace on the collar. It feels real snug on cold winter evenings but the rhinestones would be bad with plaid.

Many of my friends report the same husbandly present problem. One got a beehive with a card reading, "from your honey." Another received a grow-your-own mushroom kit. Still another, a sew-your-own sofa. (If my husband did that, I'd be tempted to give him a throw-my-own tantrum.)

When you get a strange gift from a friend, you can bury it in the basement or stash it in the attic. But when it comes from a husband, you have to find a way to hang it, sit on it, wear it, display it, or use it so he'll think you just LOOOOVE it. And then you have to "look the gift-horse in the mouth"—and smile!

Dear Lord, I'll figure out what to do with my husband. But I've discovered through the years that the strangest gifts of all come from YOU! I pick out something in the window that I think I just have to have but then you give me something totally different—and totally better. I ask for a straight path to a bright horizon and you send me on a detour with beautiful views along the way. I ask for gold and you send a sunset. I ask for jewels and you send children. I ask for earthly fame and fortune and you offer eternal happiness.

So the next time I look in my Christmas stocking and find a beehive or a banjo-shaped spittoon, a bouquet of stinkweed, or a batch of boysenberry taffy, I'll just smile and say "thank you" politely. Who knows? It could be a blessing in disguise.

10 The Snow Job in My Basement

Say it isn't snow! Say it isn't snow!

My friends have become accustomed to this lament from me; they know that I give a cold shoulder to snow. But this week was the worst yet. It's bad enough when snow shows up on my driveway, but this week it was inside my washing machine!

When I opened the door of the washer, I expected to take out what I had put in—two sheets, two pillowcases, and one pillow. Instead, the whole washer was full of this soft, fluffy, white stuff that looked just like snow. For a second, I thought Frosty the Snowman had climbed in there and self-destructed.

Evidently, there had been a tiny tear in the ticking of the pillow, unseen by me. When the tiny tear was attacked by the tumble-spin-and-mangle cycle, the pillow went all to pieces and let the washer beat the stuffing out of it. And it almost scared the stuffing out of me when I opened the door and saw the result.

After the shock wore off, I realized what had happened, pulled out the "remains" and put it aside to dry out before it went into the garbage. By the next day, when I hurried down to the basement to get it, it had dried into a soft, fluffy, white mound—and the cat was curled up in the middle of it, sound asleep. I had lost a pillow but he had found a snug snoozin' spot.

As I watched him snoozin' in the snow, I remembered the story somebody told me about a little girl and her mother who were stuck in traffic on a slippery, snowy day. The little girl said, "Mommy, when God made snow, why didn't he make it so it would fall everywhere except on the roads and driveways?"

That sounded like such a great idea to me that I wondered why God didn't think of it. But then I realized that when God made snow there were no roads or driveways—so if man wanted to mess up God's nice tidy world by adding asphalt, then man would just have to live with the results. And so would I.

I knew I should try to think positive so I thought about the people who like to ski and ice skate and build snowmen and toss snowballs. And I thought about all the people who make their living driving snowplows or working at ski resorts. The cat did not think of any of those things. He just dreamed on.

₊₊₊*₊₊*

Dear Lord, help me to remember: things that are a bane to me might be a boon to others, things that make life difficult for me might make a living for others. It all depends on your point of view. Thank you, Lord, for making a world that has room for lots of different viewpoints. Thank you for the roads I love to travel when they're not icy, and for snow cones and frozen yogurt and ice cubes and cool cloths that can soothe fevered brows like mine.

And Lord, when that cat wakes up, please don't let him drag all that pillow snow upstairs with him!

11 Don't Fence Me In!

Now I know how Tom Sawyer felt; this has been fence-painting week at my house—and I was the appointed paint person.

I tried to tell my son how much fun it was and offered to let him have a turn—and share the fun with me—but he wasn't buying. He had read the book and seen the movie. He countered and said he would cut the grass while I painted. Although I recognized the danger of ending up with a fence covered with grass-flecked paint, I agreed.

As he mowed, I sloshed and splashed away, hurrying as fast as I could to finish the job before I ran out of paint. Somehow, it didn't work out that way. Speed did not make the paint go further.

Actually, the "paint" I was using was cedar stain, a thin and splashy concoction, like Tom Sawyer's whitewash must have been. That splashiness was my excuse for polka-dotting myself as well as all the flowers and bushes.

I ran out of paint before I ran out of fence. By the time I'd splashed my last brushful, there were just a few boards left in the corner under the apple tree. I considered them thoughtfully for a few moments, then decided that the spot was so shadowy, maybe nobody would notice. Or maybe in a few days, once I was able to unbend my fingers from their paintbrush grip, I would buy some more stain and return to splash again.

Of course, if I had been able to save all the paint I'd dripped, it would have been enough to finish those last few boards. But then I couldn't have had the exclusive neighborhood rights to polka-dotted landscaping.

Just then my cedar-stained, polka-dotted muscles, which had been reaching high and bending low all afternoon, awakened from their long summer nap. And they did not wake up happily.

While I was painting myself again—this time with liniment—I began to think about how today's society seems to have gotten so good at whitewashing, at covering up, making excuses, and pointing the finger to put the blame on "somebody else—not me." Unlike Tom Sawyer's buddies, lots of people are only too willing to wield the whitewash today.

Dear Lord, what has happened to our once highly principled American conscience? Have our think muscles become too weak and sluggish to notice the whitewashing brigades that are trying to cover up injustice, inequity, immorality, and irresponsibility? Have we become too brainwashed to notice or recognize the many little whitewashed excuses that are becoming a "standard" part of everyday life? Help us, Lord. Help me. Help me to do as thorough a job of waking up my conscience as I did of waking up my arm, leg, and back muscles today! And thank you, Lord, for liniment.

12 Weeds in the Family Garden

There's a weed growing in my garden. In fact, it's growing all OVER my garden. It's relentless. It's indestructible. I love it.

I guess garden decorum dictates that I should put on my white gloves and yank out that intruder. But I can't. And it's all my mother's fault. You see, my mother had this same kind of weed growing in her garden for years. And she loved it too.

Maybe my mother and I shared a love for this particular weed because of its tenacity and cheerfulness. It is always breaking into blooms that are bluer than the sky. Whenever I catch a glimpse of all those baby blues winking up at me, I just can't help but want to smile back. So that's why I don't worry too much about the fact that my garden has gone to weed.

My mother called her weed Wandering Jude because of its traveling lifestyle—and she let it wander at will. One summer she pulled up some of it that had finally "gone too far," but then she didn't have the heart to throw it away so she planted it in a big fancy flower pot and brought it inside to bask in a sunny window. That year Jude wandered around INSIDE our house as well as outside!

That year I was also of the age to wander about, going in all directions at once. My mother let me roam but pulled ME up short too whenever I finally "went too far."

When I look at my weedy garden today, it makes me think of a friend whose son was so gifted and intelligent that he won a fine scholarship to a very prestigious university. They were so proud of him. But at the end of the first year, the boy was restless and unhappy. He gave up the scholarship and began hitchhiking around the country, doing odd jobs here and there, discovering

America and trying to discover himself. Naturally his parents were distraught. It seemed that their fine flower of a son had turned into a weed.

After a few years, though, he found a job he loved and with his creative intellect turned it into a fabulous opportunity. He went back to school at night and graduated with honors. Today he has a high-paying executive position, loves his work, and has a wonderful wife and children—a bloomin' success story in the garden of everyday life!

Dear Lord, I guess most of us have a few relatives (especially teenage ones) that we sometimes think of as weeds. And we might even be tempted to banish them from our garden. But then we look in the mirror and remember that we too have had our wandering-weed times and, through it all, you kept giving us second chances—and third and fourth chances—and still loving us all the while.

So the next time I get discouraged by my family weed patch, I'll just think of what Ralph Waldo Emerson said:

What is a weed? A plant whose virtues have not yet been discovered.

13 Tomorrow, Tomorrow...

Spring has sprung and I'm watching for the first crocus, the first robin, the first sneezy allergy attack. I'm also thinking of the coming battle with creeping crabgrass, wandering weeds, and that mean green machine of a lawn.

To make matters worse, I just looked out the window and noticed that I never did get around to putting the patio furniture away last fall. And what are those funny-looking sticks out in the back of the house? Oh yes, those are the tomato plant stakes I forgot to unstake.

With all the snowstorms, it seemed like the winter would go on forever, but where did it go? Did I sit by the fireside and read all those novels I bought at garage sales last summer? Did I knit sweaters, bake bread, write letters to long-lost friends, and do all those cozy things you're supposed to do during the long cold winter? You know the answer.

I always think "next year" will be different. I'll do all that work in winter and be ready to relax and enjoy spring. When that doesn't work out, I put on my Easter bonnet with a firm resolve to do spring housecleaning and get ready for vacation and then—suddenly, it's summer. In the good ole summertime, I plan to have lawn parties, family reunions, and get ready EARLY for the start of school but before I know it—fall has fallen.

And it's time again to bring in the patio furniture.

* * *

Dear Lord, every year spring has sprung before I have—and you let me get away with it. Even though I don't keep my promises, you always keep yours.

You still send your eternal promise—the buds on the trees, the birds on the wing, the blossoming bushes, the glorious resurrection of Easter morning. Your sun still comes up every morning, your gentle breezes still cool my brow and your friendship surrounds me and comforts me. Thank you, Lord. Remind me, Lord, that I was made in your image and—since you keep YOUR promises—I should try harder to keep mine too.

Spring has sprung. Now it's my turn.

14 A Wrinkle in Time

Seminars make me squirm. Even if the speaker is great and the subject is interesting, I feel like a kid in school and soon start to fidge. So the other day I was delighted when a seminar speaker said, "Let's take a break now. Everybody stand up and shake out the wrinkles."

What a great idea! I stood up and shook and shook but the wrinkles remained—and I'm not just talking about the ones in my skirt.

Of course, the wrinkled look in clothing has been in style lately. Stores keep advertising outfits that are supposed to be easy-care because you just wash and wear them as they are—soft and wrinkled. I guess that's what happened to my face. I washed it every day and it got soft and wrinkled and now I have to wear it that way.

But during the seminar break, I picked up some valuable information. The mention of wrinkles reminded the lady sitting next to me to share a decorating idea she had just read about. She said that when you are having a party, you should go to a discount store and buy yards and yards of muslin. Wash and dry the muslin so it will have that soft, wrinkled look. Then wrap the muslin loosely around all your furniture. Yes, that's right—you WRAP your furniture.

Then you turn all the lights off or down and put lots and lots of burning candles all over the house. This is supposed to give your home an ethereal, other-worldly look and make your guests oooh and aaah.

The idea of wrapped furniture was appealing to me because it would hide all the dents and scratches and I wouldn't have to bother dusting or polishing. And the soft lights would make my wrinkles blend in with the muslin. And maybe a party like that would not only be ethereal but spiritual. With all that soft muslin and fiery candles, I would spend the whole time PRAYING that my house wouldn't burn down!

Dear Lord, don't we humans go to a lot of trouble just to get a few oohs and aahs? And don't we go to a lot of trouble worrying about foolish things like wrinkles? Every new plateau, every new surprise adds another furrow to the brow.

But, Lord, I know YOU know all about that. You have sent me such wonderful gifts, such exciting opportunities to change and still I hesitate. I tremble with fear instead of placing my hand in yours and stepping forth. I worry about "what if," debate whether "now or later or never," seesaw back and forth between CAN and can't. Forgive me, Lord. Help me to trust in you and have confidence in myself. And, Lord, if I wrap up all my insecurities instead of my furniture and promise to try to accept the new wrinkles in my life with more gumption, will you please stop putting all those new wrinkles in my face?

15 Sink or Swim

When I go swimming, it is not a pretty sight. Some little children take one look at me, shriek, and head for the other end of the pool. Other children follow me around, staring. And I don't blame them. Since I hate to get water in my nose, I wear a strange black noseclip that makes me look like a walrus.

It all started when I took my first swimming lesson. We didn't live near water when I was a child so I never learned. And when I was a teenager, I was non-liberated enough to think that all a girl was supposed to do at a pool was sit around in a new bathing suit, trying to hold her tummy in and keep her hair (and her suit) dry. Finally, as a young adult, I decided to take the plunge and enrolled in a swim class.

At "graduation" time, when all the other students were valiantly paddling across the pool, I had just gotten brave enough to float on my back—but not my front. Determined, I re-enrolled and took the same class a second time.

By now the instructor had noticed I did not like to get water in my nose and presented me with a wonderful gift—THE noseclip. This was not a dainty, skin-colored clip like they sell in sporting goods stores. It had two thick black rubber pads that fit at each side of the nose and they were joined by an ominous-looking silvery wire coil that went under the nose and acted like a spring to keep your nostrils glued shut.

It looked like it might have been the nose decoration of an African tribal dancer at an ancient voodoo ceremony. And maybe that's what it was because when I wore that clip, it worked magic.

It looked so forbidding that the water parted like the Red Sea and never a drop dared think of entering my nose. Soon I was swimming across the pool like the rest of the class. I was so inspired that I continued into the intermediate class and even beyond. Eventually, I could even jump off the side of the pool and swim laps. It was a miracle!

In all the years since, I have treasured my noseclip the way others treasure Grandma's silver service. I never leave home for the pool without it. I get into the pool with it, and while the kids are staring, the adults are snickering, and the lifeguard is watching me suspiciously. I often wished I knew where that teacher got the clip so I could get a spare but I never found another like it.

Then one year we went sightseeing in Chicago. At a museum, we toured a real enemy submarine captured in World War II. Along with other artifacts from the sub, prominently displayed for all to see was a big black noseclip just like mine! I've been trying ever since to convince my son that I am NOT old enough to have been a WWII secret agent!

Dear Lord, forgive me for being so dependent on that silly nose clip. I could probably swim just as well without it but I don't want to try. I guess there are a lot of other things that I cling to, foolishly thinking I couldn't survive without them. I know I could, Lord, I just don't want to try. I guess I'm lazy, Lord. It's so comfortable to have something familiar to hang on to and depend on. Help me, Lord, to be less dependent on "things" and more dependent on you. But please let me keep that noseclip, Lord—it's so much fun to be the only walrus in the pool!

16 My House Is Falling Apart—and So Am I!

Everything at my house is falling apart, including me. All my friendly household helpers have suddenly lost their Christian attitudes. They have decided it is more blessed to shirk than to work.

Has this ever happened at your house?

First the air conditioner issued a cease-and-desist order and lost its cool. It kept blowing air through the house, but it was HOT air, and this family already has more than enough of that!

Next, the dishwasher started leaving bits of grit on all the dishes. Gritting our teeth became an unhappy surprise at every family meal.

Then the garage door started acting funny. It already LOOKED funny because the bottom wood panel had what we delicately called spot-rot. We thought we had that problem solved when a handyman said he could fix it easily. He "fixed" it all right! The new panel he installed was so heavy that the electric garage-door opener huffed and puffed and strained only a few times, trying to lift it, before it filed a complaint about unfair working conditions and went on strike. Now we needed a new door AND a new opener.

And when our old refrigerator saw the younger workers lying down on the job, it realized how tired it was and put in for a pension.

Trying to find the money to replace all these household helpers is bad enough, but shopping for them is almost worse!

I have heard so many conflicting stories about "best buys," energy efficiency, and product reliability that I have started wondering how it would be to just have a fan, a dishpan, a horse, and an ice box!

* * * * *

Dear Lord, the work stoppage at my house has made me feel like striking, too—anything and anybody who comes near! I am also in the mood to shirk instead of work! I look around and see other people who seem to work less and enjoy life more and I want to head for the couch to spend the day with a good book and a box of chocolates.

Well, Lord, you and I know that some days—when nobody is looking—I give myself permission to do just that! But most days I face up to reality, put on my work face and get down to business.

Lord, thank you for giving me the freedom to take an occasional day off, and thank you for the opportunity to work, to achieve, and to contribute. Help me to remember, Lord, that success is not GETTING the best you can, but GIVING the best you can. And, Lord, could you please pass that message along to my household helpers?

17 Furrowed Eyebrows

Did you know that cats don't have eyebrows? I never spent much time thinking about that until one night I heard a TV comic making jokes about how silly cats look without eyebrows.

The next time my cat stared soulfully into my face (as he often does), I stared back and discovered it's true—no eyebrows. The poor little thing only has three funny-looking whiskers standing straight up on each side of his forehead. This means he can't knit his brows, have a furrowed brow, or raise an eyebrow in surprise or amazement. He can't even frown!

Of course, he can't smile either. Now is that any way to go through life?

But cats have learned—as we all should—that any difficulty can be overcome. Even without eyebrows, my cat can perfectly convey anger, fear, suspicion, and total disgust—and he can shoot all those looks right across the room at my husband.

Since my husband HAS eyebrows, he shoots the looks right back. For a few minutes, we have a shootout in the family room corral. It's usually a draw.

Then my husband returns to reading his paper and our brave kittycat minces around the edge of the room, far away from the other shooter, leaps into my lap and purrs happily, satisfied with his latest skirmish. He has accomplished his mission without the ability to frown. And when you can purr, who needs to smile ?

* * * * *

Dear Lord, a lot of people pass up really great opportunities because they think they have a lack. They say "I can't" to every situation because they don't have the looks, the brains, the training, the education, the money, or whatever they think is absolutely necessary to accomplish the task.

I know one of those people very well. I see her every morning in the mirror while I am brushing my teeth. She is often groaning and mumbling, "I have ten things too many to do today. I'll never get it all done. I know I can't. I know I can't...."

Yes, Lord, I'm guilty. I get weak-in-the-knees and weak-in-the-head, worrying instead of working. I know you gave us all different talents and abilities. I know I can't climb the highest mountain, catch a shooting star, or even bake the best banana cake. But I also know you are on my side, Lord, and you will help me through every day—even those days when I have "furrowed eyebrows."

18 The Closet Caper

I'm so excited. I just learned that my son's closet has been declared an historic landmark!

Oh, I don't mean his current closet—the one with all the baseball cards and the prehistoric tennis shoes and the nice ties he's never worn and the good suit he outgrew two years ago and the cage for the gerbil that died three years ago. No, that closet could only be declared a city landfill.

The historic closet is in the apartment where we lived when we were first married. That first home was full of challenges. The living room was long and skinny and I spent a year rearranging the furniture, sure that I would find a way to make it look fatter and friendlier. I never did.

The biggest conversation piece in the place was the hall closet. That closet was bigger than the kitchen and about half as big as our bedroom—and it had two doors, which made it the only room in the apartment that had cross-ventilation! When our son was born, it seemed only logical to turn such a choice location into his nursery.

We painted it and decorated it and moved in a chest of drawers and a crib and a fluffy white music box lamb that played a lullaby. All our friends were either amused or aghast. We were the only ones with a closet kid.

But he lived there happily until we could save enough money to move into a small house where he could have a real room of his own.

Through the years, I would occasionally drive by our former home to take a nostalgic look. It had begun to deteriorate. One day, I drove past and saw that it was empty with the windows boarded up and all the beautiful flower beds gone. It was like running into an old friend who has fallen upon hard times. I grieved a bit as I looked through the photo album and remembered the happy times we had spent there. And then today there was this big article in the paper with a photo of the building as I remembered it, announcing that it is to be rehabbed and reborn.

I don't know why it was declared "historic" unless someone told them about our nursery closet, but I'm happy to know that now some new families can enjoy its old-world charm and its cross-ventilated closets!

Dear Lord, thank you for all the joyful times in that old building. We had so little money in those days—but so much fun and so much hope for the future. Please help all the couples just starting out today, Lord—the ones who don't know any better yet, the ones who think you have to start with a big beautiful new house, two new cars, and enough money for fancy vacations. And remind me again, Lord, to appreciate all the small blessings in my life, to be aware that I don't need lots of "things" to make a closet full of memories.

19 True Treasures

Rockefeller had his millions. Elizabeth Taylor her diamonds. And Julia Child her French recipes.

But those are just ordinary grown-up treasures. What about childhood treasures? How about a big cardboard refrigerator box? Now, my friends, we are talking TRUE TREASURE!

Today, as I was driving through my subdivision, I spotted—right in the middle of a perfectly manicured lawn—a couple of kids playing in a refrigerator box with a "door" cut in the side. Their fancy walking, talking, computerized toys had been abandoned as they journeyed on the wings of imagination. I knew the future of the world was safe.

Just the sight of that box brought back a flood of memories about my own "magic" box. Now you must understand that these boxes—like all treasures—are not easy to obtain. You cannot go into a toy store and buy one or order one from a toll-free number. It has to arrive at your house, wrapped around a large new appliance. And even parents who love to redecorate do not buy too many new refrigerators in the course of one childhood.

Fortunately, my parents got one just in time to save me from an underprivileged youth. The minute I inherited the box, the neighborhood kids and I took it to our hearts and prayed every night for a long drought so our treasure would be safe from damaging rain.

We did have some showers that summer but the sheltering limbs of a huge tree and the after-rain summer sun kept the box safe. And we used it for a castle, a fortress, a mansion, a theater, or whatever we could imagine until fall came and we went back to school and the box went to wherever old refrigerator boxes go. (My parents always protected me from such unsettling information and evidently whisked the box into the garbage while I was at school.)

Years later, my son had "his" box—and he and his friends were more careful than we had been. They managed to drag their box down the stairs to the basement where it was safe from the elements. And it lasted for years. First, it was a secret clubhouse. Then it became a rocket ship in which they blasted off to planets still uncharted. Then it turned into a laboratory where they invented what they considered diabolical devices. With the addition of miles of string, rolls of adding machine tape (found at a garage sale), and broken bits of toys, the box was transformed into a new wonder every week.

We took our son and his friends to the park, the zoo, the planetarium, the museums. We enjoyed picnics, field trips, vacations, and even Disney World. But his most treasured memory—and mine—is the "box."

..*.*.*.*.*

Dear Lord, thanks for such happy days and happy memories. Help me and all of today's "sophisticated" adults to remember how much joy can be found in simple things by using your gifts of creativity and imagination. Help us be careful to not let today's lavish expectations and expensive "toys" rob us—and our children—of the joy of "unscheduled" time to dream and invent, of the innocence and wonder that can turn an empty box into a magic carpet.

20 Life Is Just a Bowl of Peaches

Everything's been peachy at my house recently. And it's driving me bananas!

Our freezer's so full of frozen peaches that there's little room for any other frozen assets. Our refrigerator's so full of stewed peaches and peach jam that there's little room for ham and bologna (both of which have long been staples in this family). And our tummies are so full of peach pies, peach cobblers, and peach "surprises" that we are ready to join Peaches Anonymous.

It all started about a month ago. The two little peach trees in our backyard have always been a particular delight to me. They never have expected me to give them special food, water, care, or even conversation. They just have waited there quietly every year to blossom forth in spring and fruit forth in summer with a small harvest of outrageously delicious peaches. We would eat the peaches fresh from the tree, make some peach pies, and share a few with neighbors.

But last year, a spring frost hit at the height of peach-blooming season so there was not one peach on either tree. I moaned and groaned all summer about no peaches being the pits. This year I've been moaning and groaning for a different reason. Those two little trees seemed determined to make up for last year's fruitlessness. They blossomed forth with so much fruit that their branches sagged to the ground. Suddenly one day, they began to bombard me in bushels and pecks until I had peaches up to my neck!

At first, I was so pleased playing Farmer Brown, carrying in my crop every day, peeling and pitting and freezing and baking. But then the harvest began to get ahead of me. No matter how many I gave away or how fast I peeled, those peaches seemed to multiply overnight. I began to realize that too much of a good thing could be too much. I'm in the pits again!

49

* * * * *

Dear Lord, forgive me if I seem ungrateful. I still love those little trees and I'm grateful to have fruit free for the picking and the pitting. But Lord, this has made me think about how some other peachy things in life can also turn into pitfalls. Chocolate is good for the taste buds but too much is bad for the poundage. Television can be wonderfully entertaining but too much numbs sensitivity and dumbs imagination. Material possessions are nice to have but too many can enslave.

And freedom. Ah, fabulous freedom. We all long for it, wait for it as youngsters, demand it as teenagers. But when we get it, sometimes it's so overwhelming we don't know what to do with it. Thank you, Lord, for giving me freedom to choose the work I will do, the dreams I will dream, the life I will lead. But please give me guidance too, Lord. Help me to avoid the pits and the pitfalls and use my freedom wisely in this pitted but peachy world of yours.

21 Out on a Limb of the Family Tree

This summer we lost a close family friend. Our Russian olive tree bit the dust when all its leaves left.

It was close because it was planted at the edge of the patio, right outside our kitchen window. It was a friend because it provided cooling shade for the kitchen and a handy landing pad for the birds in the summer. It was always one of the first signs of springtime, with its fluffy little flowers. And in the fall, its hard, green, olive-like berries seemed to be a popular bird snack. It did its bit in the winter too when ice or snow turned its graceful branches into a lacy frame for the view from the window in our family room.

Still, I complained about it. Why? Because every time I stepped onto the patio there was a new chore for me to do—thanks to my friendly tree.

As soon as I would sweep up the litter from its springtime blossoms, the breeze would blow down another batch to put my broom back into action. Then the falling olives would need sweeping too because they were hard and round enough to turn an ankle, turning a grin into a grimace.

And those straggly limbs! The friendly tree insisted on reaching over path and fence, forever threatening to snag an unwary visitor with a thorny tickle. So even in the winter, I would find myself out there trimming limbs and trying to jam their uneven thorniness into garbage cans.

So why did I put up with it all these years? Because I loved it, of course. It was a lot of trouble but it gave us blossoms and shade and branches for bird friends. It couldn't help the fact that it came equipped with thorns and falling olives. It just did what God made it to do.

In fact, it even grew higher and lasted longer than most trees of its kind. That's why there was a tear in my eye when the buzz-saw had to chop it down. And now, every time I look out the window, the patio just doesn't seem right. It's neater but emptier. My broom and I are getting a rest. But I miss my troublesome family friend.

Dear Lord, my tree was a lot like a family tree. Children can't help causing a lot of trouble when they are babies. They can't help the fact that they need feeding and burping and changing and rocking. And as they grow, they make so many messes for us to clean up that it's easy to get irritated with them and complain all the time.

But as soon as they go away to school or get married or move into their own apartments, the house just doesn't seem the same without them. It's neater but emptier. And lonelier.

Thank you, Lord, for all the troublesome little sprouts and the growing pains of our family tree. Forgive all the complaining and show all us adults how to do as much giggling as griping, realizing that some day we're gonna miss the mess!

22 Bye Bye Ballpoint, Hello Eraser!

If only I could learn to write my life in pencil so I could erase the mistakes!

Last week I was in the dentist's office and his hygienist was trying to rearrange appointments to fit in an emergency patient. When she found a way to "erase" one patient and pencil in the other, she laughingly explained that that was why she kept records in pencil.

Suddenly it dawned on me that that was what I had been doing wrong all these years—never living in pencil so I could erase!

Unfortunately, I have always been good at making scenes and spectacles that could never be erased from others' memories—or mine. I have also been known to make loud, never-to-be-taken-back statements and proclamations about what I absolutely would or would not do in my future life—only to find myself hard-pressed to live up to the bluster.

For example, I can remember when my sister was a young mother with a toddler in tow and I was a footloose single know-it-all. Whenever she would or would not discipline her son, I would think, "I would never, ever, as long as I live, treat my child like that." A few years later, I found myself treating my child EXACTLY like that.

I can remember when I was a teenager and whatever my mother said, did, suggested, or planned, I would think, "I would never, ever, as long as I live, do ANYthing like that." Now I find myself speaking, doing, suggesting, and planning many of the exact same things she did.

I can remember when my friends married earlier than I did

and always arrived at our get-togethers with snapshots and stories of their children's latest exploits. I would think I would never, ever, as long as I lived, bore other people with "cute" anecdotes. But as soon as my son arrived, I too began recounting stories of the "little darling" to friends, relatives, and total strangers I met at a party or in line at the grocery.

And I hate to even think about the many times I have announced that for the rest of my life—through rain, snow, sleet, attacks of killer locusts, avalanches, and falling stars—I will stay on a diet, keep the basement clean, and put all family photos in an album.

Where is that eraser when I need one?

..*.*.*

Dear Lord, help! I've got to get rid of the indelible pen and learn the art of erasing. Please help me to remove foot from mouth and put some prayers in there instead. Help me to be less judgmental and more "mental." Remind me to think before I speak, and pray before I proclaim. Help me to work on myself instead of others. Then, if I can't find an erasable personal pencil, at least I can get the lead out!

23 Double-Time, Double Takes, and Double Jeopardy

My cat is leading a double life. At home, he meekly sits by the fireside, napping and purring, a picture of contentment and tranquility. Sometimes he curls up in my lap, keeping one eye half-open, just in case an intruder (like my husband) should appear. Other times, he quietly munches the cat yummies from his little bowl in a kitchen corner or sits staring out the window, keeping his feline feelings to himself.

But when he goes OUT, that's a different story. He steps through the patio door and turns into Adventure Cat. He scampers across the lawn, sharpens his claws on the big oak, then lurks in the bushes, crouched like a lion, pretending to guard our backyard. He climbs our trees and has been known to leap our tall rooftop in a single bound.

No wonder we're such good friends. He reminds me a little of myself—or any other "working woman" who leads a double life. We, too, sometimes sit meekly by the fireside, napping and purring, with one eye open to what's going on around us. We, too, quietly munch our diet meals of celery, carrot sticks, and chocolate bars in a kitchen corner (so no one will notice there's more chocolate than carrots!). We, too, give the appearance of contentment and tranquility. But when we go OUT—that's a different story.

The moment a woman steps through her front door on her way to work, she is expected to transform herself into Executive Woman! She must be alert, efficient, well-informed, and well-dressed, prepared to make decisions instantly and logically (not sentimentally) and able to leap every crisis in a single bound.

If she is a stay-at-home working woman, she must transform herself into a whirl of efficiency the minute she steps out her front door to assume her roles as chairperson of committees, coordinator of school or church activities, leader of Girl Scouts, president of social clubs, or general-in-charge of a myriad of other worthwhile posts.

In addition to keeping the homefires burning and setting the world on fire, women always seem to have those endless little chores and errands to run—trips to the cleaners, gas station, drugstore, hardware store, grocery store. Oh yes, always and forever, trips to the grocery store.

Somehow this double life doesn't seem as much fun as climbing trees or flying across rooftops, but at least there's never a dull moment—because we never know when an emergency will strike and Executive Woman must charge forth to the rescue!

_ *_* *_* *

Dear Lord, I guess I should stop spending so much time complaining about this double life and realize that's the way the world is today. This is my culture, my era, the way my world operates. Help me, Lord, to understand that but not just accept it as is. Help me to keep trying to improve it and make it better for myself and for my family.

Remind me, Lord, of that Chinese proverb: "A wise person learns to adapt to circumstances as water shapes itself to the vessel that contains it." Teach me, Lord, to adapt but not to settle. Help me to keep trying to beautify this vessel—and to appreciate and enjoy the double blessings in this double life.

24 Vinegar Pie and Corncob Jelly

Had any cabbage cake at your house this week? How about vinegar pie, tomato soup cake, or cold oven pound cake? Don't laugh. I have recipes for all of them and—believe it or not—they're delicious.

Of course, the folks at my house are no longer surprised at the strange things that show up on our dinner table. When you grow up in the South, as I did, you believe in dishes like corn pudding, scrivels, kidney beans with dumplings, crackling bread, and red-eye gravy. My husband has never learned to really "believe in" those things—but he's no longer surprised by them.

The tomato soup cake (my mother's recipe) comes out a lovely shade of pink and is topped with a fluffy cream-cheese frosting. The cold oven pound cake was my aunt's recipe and the vinegar pie was my grandmother's. But the cabbage cake idea came from an old cookbook that has recipes for things that even my relatives never served.

How about scalded-meal muffins, pot-liquor dodgers (cornbread cakes cooked on top of a pot of spring greens), rinktum tiddy (made with tomatoes and melted cheese and served on crackers—a forerunner of today's nachos with cheese), bird-nest pudding (made with apples and spices), black pepper cookies, and corncob jelly (they actually boiled a bunch of red corncobs, then strained the juice and mixed it with sugar and pectin)!

The housewives of today have no idea how much their foremothers had to improvise. Just think about all that grinding, boiling, straining—and imagining. It took a lot of creativity to figure out a way to feed your family by concocting recipes using vinegar, black pepper, and corncobs.

But maybe their best recipe of all was the one for a happy home. Families of those days worked together. And if they didn't have a lot, they "made do"—a talent that many of today's families seem to have lost.

Recently, I read an article about financial planning that suggested ways for families to plan now to accumulate a "fortune" for the future. But the article must have been written by someone who once ate vinegar pie, because it ended by saying something like this: "If you don't think you're ever really going to have a 'fortune,' is that so terrible? Is it possible you could be happy with one color TV, one car, a well-stocked refrigerator, a small but comfortable home, hot and cold running water, and a secure if modest future?"

The article ended by saying, "One way to get rich is to win the lottery or inherit a million dollars. Another way is to need less."

Need less! What a rich idea!

₊₊*₊*₊*

Dear Lord, no matter how much we get today, we keep thinking we need more. Forgive us, Lord. The middle class in America today lives like royalty did in the past. We take for granted such things as supermarkets with an unlimited supply of fresh fruit, vegetables, and meat—while people in other countries stand in line just to buy a loaf of bread. Yet we think we need MORE. Thank you, Lord, for all our riches. Help us to recognize them. Show us again how to value the talent to "make do," need less, and appreciate life's simpler pleasures—like vinegar pie and corncob jelly.

25 I Do, You Do, They Did What?

" An archeologist is the best husband a woman can have—the older she gets, the more interested he is in her." That fascinating quote came from the famous mystery writer, Agatha Christie, who was married to an archeologist. Unfortunately, my husband is not an archeologist. But he DOES love history; maybe he will find me more interesting the more "historical" I become!

When I found that Christie quote in a book about wedding trivia, I also discovered that traditions through the years have not always been kind to the bride.

The ancient Romans had a tradition that was downright crummy. After the wedding, they would break the cake over the bride's head! The guests would gather up the crumbs for good luck but the bride would leave for her honeymoon with stars in her eyes and icing in her eyelashes.

The custom of the many-layered wedding cake we enjoy today began in pioneer days when the wedding was a popularity contest for the poor bride. The wedding guests would each bring a layer of cake and the layers would be filled with applesauce and stacked—and the popularity of the bride was judged by how tall her cake was!

Then in 1747, in an effort to protect "gullible" grooms, someone passed a law against the blushing bride wearing blush or ANY kind of makeup. The marriage might not be considered legal if the husband had been "ensnared" by the "illusion" of makeup.

Evidently even brides with pale cheeks and short cakes were in demand because the custom of the bride standing to the left of the groom at the altar began so the groom's right hand would be free if necessary to draw his sword and fight off jealous rivals!

My wedding was perfect of course (!) but it must have been non-traditional. My husband did not wear a sword and there was no applesauce in the cake and no cake in my hair. But we DID both have blushing cheeks when it came time for the after-ceremony kiss. And that custom DOES have an interesting history.

Since the letter X is the first letter of the Greek word for Christ and X also stands for the cross, in the Middle Ages, it became the Christian custom for people to sign a contract with an X. Even kings and queens who knew how to write a signature signed with an X as a symbol of good faith.

To further guarantee the sincerity of their intentions and to ensure that they would live up to the promises in the contract, they would kiss the signature. This became known as the "kiss of truth" and was the beginning of the phrase, "sealed with a kiss."

Soon it became the custom at a wedding for the couple to kiss as a sign of the sincerity of their intentions to live up to the promises of the wedding contract—whether the husband was an archeologist or not!

Dear Lord, today when so many families are struggling, help marriage partners to work faithfully together to build stronger bonds and happier families. In our "instant" society, remind us that it takes time to work through problems and it takes patience to continue to appreciate each other through better or worse, through aging and changing. And Lord, even though some of those customs sound silly, thank you for all the beautiful traditions we have that make our celebrations memorable and meaningful—and fun too!

26 Money Is the Root of All Upheaval

My son finally found a summer job. That's the good news. The wait-a-minute news is that his making money is gonna cost US plenty!

He found one of those wonderful healthy jobs with lots of fresh air, sunshine, exercise, activity—and dirt! After a day like that, when he comes home, he no longer drops his clothes on the floor. Now he can just stand them in the corner!

This means good ole Mom can pre-soak, re-soak, wash, re-wash, and wring her hands along with the clothes—but the stains, grease, and paint still won't come out. It's a dirty job, so Mom gets to do it!

Of course, those hopelessly stained and faded clothes will probably have to be replaced before school starts. And we know that a few extra tons of bleach and detergent can get expensive. So by the end of the summer, his laundry is gonna take our budget to the cleaners!

But the wash/rinse cycle is nothing compared to the lunch/supper cycle. Do you know what fresh air does to a growing boy's appetite?! Every day he suggests adding just one more thing to his bulging lunchbox to "tide him over" to suppertime. Pretty soon, fixing his lunch will take about as much time as packing a picnic for a family reunion! And supper! I'm beginning to understand how farm ladies feel when they cook for a bunch of hired hands at harvest time.

Oh well, I know I should rejoice because he's getting all that fresh air and sunshine and I'm grateful that he has a job, ANY job. After all, I was the one who kept praying in the dark of winter, asking God to help with the job search for the heat of summer. And besides, I've always heard it takes money to make money. Now I know what that means.

Unfortunately, family money is sort of like a summer shower. Even when it comes down fast, it dries up in a hurry.

You get a tax refund, but before you can deposit it, the lawn mower dies. The dentist says the kids have no expensive cavities but on the way home from his office, the car breaks down. You finally get some money saved for a rainy day and the roof springs a leak. Or your kid gets a summer job.

₊₊*₊*₊*

Dear Lord, I know that somehow it always works out and the money stretches and the rain makes the flowers grow and climbing the rainbow is fun even when there's a pot of beans at the end instead of a pot of gold! Help me remember that as I teeter-totter on the brink, trying to achieve a well-balanced checkbook, outlook, and life. Remind me of what a wisecracker once said, "Most money is tainted. 'Tain't yours and 'tain't mine."

Thank you, Lord, for my son's summer job. But please make autumn fall quickly—before his tainted income bankrupts us!

27 Tell Your Lilacs to Go Play in Traffic!

This year, I discovered one of the secrets of the Green Thumb Club: lilacs like traffic.

Horticulturists may disagree, but I have proof. It all began several years ago when I carefully planted a lilac bush in what I considered a perfect spot in my backyard. It grew into a large green plant, which was nice. But what I wanted were those lacy, sweet-smelling lilac flowers that perfume the springtime.

Friends kept telling me that it takes a long time for lilacs to bloom and to wait and be patient. I was patient for eight years.

When we moved to a new house, I almost went off and left the lilac in the lurch, but finally I dug it up and dragged it along. In its new backyard, it grew again into a bush with no flowers.

The next year we put up a new fence and the lilac was in the way so I transplanted it again. Two years later, a big evergreen out front died and when we dug it out there was a nice big hole—ready to be filled. I didn't have another bush on hand and the lilac was in the backyard where another hole wouldn't matter so we transplanted it again.

It was a bad day for transplanting—hot and dry. My son and I started out digging carefully, trying not to break the roots—but the hotter it got, the faster we dug. Finally, we yanked out the roots, dumped them in the hole and hoped for the best.

Obviously, I had been too polite to that lilac in the past because the next spring what had been a nice green bush all those years turned into a nice green bush with TWO blossoms!

When I saw the blooms, I ran into the house screaming and shouting about something wonderful happening. My husband thought we must have won a million-dollar lottery. He was just a

LITTLE disappointed when I told him about the two lilac blooms.

But the best was yet to come. This spring, the lilac bush was absolutely covered with fragrant flowers, just as a lilac bush is supposed to be. And there could be only one explanation—lilacs like traffic.

All those years the lilac had been in a backyard. When I finally moved it to the front, right by the side of the garage where it could watch the traffic and inhale the gas fumes, it choked, gasped, and bloomed!

Dear Lord, that lilac reminds me of children. Sometimes we expect them to grow in the backyard of our life, with just an occasional pat on the head and a birthday hug. And many do just fine that way. But other children need a little extra. Like the lilac, they just can't seem to bloom where they were planted. They need a different kind of atmosphere, attention, or situation.

Sometimes a parent has to keep "moving them about," tugging at their roots, putting them in a different school or activity, suggesting new projects or possibilities to help them find a bloom-able spot in life. The secret—as with most things—is patience, endurance, and careful attention. If one thing doesn't work, try another. Never give up. That's the way you treated me, isn't it, Lord? You've tugged at my roots a lot. I was a late bloomer but you never gave up on me. Thank you, Lord, for paying attention.

28 Playing the Word Game

I only speak one foreign language—English. It seems foreign at times because there are so many words that are pronounced the same but spelled differently, words that are spelled the same but have totally different meanings, and words that are both of the above.

I know the difference between road, rode, and rowed. I know about be and bee, sea and see, flee and flea. Yes, I speak a foreign language. But my son, the word merchant, computer scientist, and expert on the world-at-large continues to try to educate me about word usage.

One day we saw a sign that read, "Sale on 1-inch window blinds." My son informed me that they would never sell because no one has a 1-inch window. Another day we noticed a truck with the name of a company that does "furniture stripping." My son informed me they would surely go out of business because no one would pay to have furniture stripped of drawer pulls, handles, knobs, trims, etc.

On second thought, he speculated that maybe the company did furniture stripping the way you do weatherstripping: filling in all the cracks, putting putty or tape on every crevice, making it all airtight. But then, of course, people wouldn't want that either because they wouldn't be able to open a dresser drawer or slide open a sliding door on a bookcase or get into the kitchen cabinets. So, just as he suspected at first, the company was doomed to bankruptcy.

But the day we were discussing computer language was even worse. I don't speak "computer" very well but he is fluent in it so I was wide open to his slings and slurs. I had thought RAM was a large sheep but he informed me it's Random Access Memory. I had thought a warm start was having a cup of coffee before you left the house and a cold start was having to shovel snow before you could get out of the driveway. He explained to me they were methods of "booting" (turning on) the computer.

Then he told me to hit a certain computer key. When I did, the screen filled with strange symbols and unattached letters that looked like a message sent to King Tut. Reacting with panic, I screeched, "That's crazy. I can't read that." Calmly and maturely, my son said, "It's crazy because YOU can't read it? If you picked up a book that was written in German, would you say it was crazy just because YOU couldn't read it?"

I shot the smart-alecky kid a motherly sneer and returned to my lesson. He had hit a nerve.

Dear Lord, how often I DO think something is crazy just because I don't understand it. When confronted with a new way of doing things, a new viewpoint, a new possibility, I often decry it before I try it. Thank you, Lord, for these "consciousness-raising" sessions with my son. They widen my horizons, give me a younger outlook, make me think—and drive me crazy! Actually, they're sort of like some sessions I've had with you, Lord. You also do some strange things to my life that I don't understand and therefore dispute. Forgive me, Lord, for too often falling in hate at first sight. Help me, Lord, to learn to speak my son's language—AND yours!

29 Best-Laid Plans

I never liked the Midwest. I never daydreamed of living near the banks of the Mississippi, on a flood plain. I always thought I would live in Hawaii, Hollywood, Paris, or somewhere along the yellow brick road or over the rainbow.

So, of course, I live in the Midwest.

I didn't plan it that way. I started out in a small Southern town and worked at a lot of little jobs but always with my eyes on a prize—an exciting job that could lead me to a glamorous life in a faraway, fabulous part of the world. Finally, I found the exciting job in a faraway town—in the Midwest, near the banks of the Mississippi, on a flood plain.

But it was a wonderful, challenging job. I soon learned to love the sights, the sounds, the opportunities, and the people of the Midwest. I found many delightful new friends—AND a handsome husband!

I didn't want to live in the Midwest, but I'm sure glad I do.

I never liked Japanese cars. I thought others looked more sporty and exciting and cars made closer to home would be more dependable and easier to get repaired. And besides, anybody who talks to a car as much as I do shouldn't have one that speaks a foreign language.

So, of course, I have a Japanese car.

I didn't plan it that way. When I decided my old beat-up jalopy needed a retirement plan, I went shopping for a bright new American-made car that would give me good gas mileage and a better image. I found some great cars that had everything I was looking for—except the price tag. Then I went shopping for a USED car with a more friendly price tag.

One day I stopped at a used-car lot, took one look at a "previously owned" jazzy Japanese car with silver spoke wheels and a sun roof, and knew it was "mine." I tried to resist. I tried to find some fault when I took it for a test drive but everything was perfect. I knew I might as well buy it or it would follow me home.

Since then, we have happily traveled the road together with very few repair bills and very many miles to the gallon.

I never liked the idea of being a stay-at-home housewife—a job that required cooking and cleaning, discipline and diplomacy. I thought I was more suited to be a movie star, astronaut, or self-made millionaire.

So, of course, I became a housewife. And lived scrappily but happily ever after.

Dear Lord, I guess you knew I needed a Midwestern town to "center" me, a foreign car instead of a foreign locale, and the title "housewife" to keep my nose to the grindstone and out of international politics. You DO have a way of changing my best-laid plans. Thank you, Lord, for your better-laid plans. Every day I am reminded of that beautiful meditation, "I got nothing I asked for but everything I hoped for. I am among all people most richly blessed." And I rejoice.

27 Brown Bag Banter

Brown-bagging is not my bag. Even when I was a kid, I could not get excited about spending noontime with a little sack that held a soggy sandwich, crumbled cookies, and a bruised banana.

But in recent years, the brown bag has become fashionable, or at least acceptable. Even executives have been seen opening their briefcases to reveal a brief lunch encased in a brown bag. They have discovered that "eating in" is faster, less expensive, and lets you count your own calories.

All those benefits make brown-bagging practical and reasonable—so that's probably why I don't like the custom. Practicality and reasonableness have never played prominent parts in my lifestyle. But I DO get a chuckle every time I see a brown bag because of the time a friend tried to use a brown bag for medical purposes.

He had been having a problem with hyperventilation, so the doctor said the next time had trouble breathing, he should put a brown bag over his head for a few minutes. Evidently that's a routine suggestion to help with such a problem.

One day my friend brought donuts to the office for breakfast and left the empty bag sitting on his desk. Later in the morning, he felt a breathing attack coming on and grabbed up the donut bag and put it over his head. As he sat at his desk with a bag on his head and powdered sugar sifting over his shoulders, the boss brought in an important client to meet his "star" employee. The scene made a big impression on boss and client—but it was not a good career move.

Every time I remember that story I think about how paper bags are a lot like people. You can't judge what's inside by the way they look on the outside. Two bags can look pretty much alike. But inside one you might find powdered donuts, inside the other, expensive imported caviar. You have to look inside to tell the difference. And even then, you have to judge for yourself which is better—the donuts or the caviar.

It's so easy to take people at "face value"—to never try to see inside to learn what makes them tick or makes them hurt.

It's so easy to allow others to maintain that bag-over-the-head look—especially if you are hiding under your own bag!

｡｡*｡*｡*

Dear Lord, I am one of the bag people. I sometimes hide behind my own false face, keeping others away, never letting them come close enough to see my hurts and hopes. And I let my friends get away with the same trick. Help me to change that, Lord. Help me to start seeing my friends as old bags. No, no, that's not quite right!... Help me to get to know my baggy friends better—and allow them to know me better too.

But, Lord, if you see me sitting in a corner with a bag over my head, don't worry. I'm probably not hiding or having trouble breathing. I'm probably just trying to get that last bit of powdered sugar from the morning donuts!

31 Stressed and Undressed Furniture

The naked eye, the naked truth, the naked city. Yes, I've heard of all those—but naked furniture?

The other day, I stopped at a red light alongside a truck with a huge sign on its side that advertised just that—"Naked Furniture."

It took me a few seconds to realize that the sign referred to UNPAINTED furniture! Then I began to think about all the naked furniture in our house. There's the yellow bookcase that has a lot of naked places where the paint has been nicked off by years of book satchels being tossed on it, keys being dropped on it and toy cars being raced into it.

The bedroom furniture has a few naked nicks and notches that I tried to "fix" with the help of a brown crayon. The magazine article I read said that a brown crayon would work every time—but I guess nothing works every time. So I decided the only answer was "subdued" lighting and put 40-watt bulbs in that room.

Even our living room—where things are a bit more formal—has some naked spots. The coffee table has a few tiny tooth-prints that weren't put there by the dog.

But there is actually only one piece of furniture in the house that ever got to the point where it needed a bathrobe to cover its naked wood—the old chest in the family room. When we first got married, I dragged that chest out of somebody's basement and painted it pink. It seemed like a good idea at the time.

After a few years, being "in the pink" didn't seem so cute any more and the poor old chest got dragged to OUR basement.

But one day I felt real ambitious and decided "something could be done with it." Off to the hardware store I trotted for some paint-stripper and soon I was elbow-deep in oozing pink paint and gooey stripper.

Since I had never done that kind of job before—and never will again—I expected the naked wood to have a rich, warm shine with honeyed golden undertones like the beautiful old furniture I see in antique stores. Wrong! It only looked like a boring board.

On a return trip to the hardware store, I was told it was up to me to add a finish and rub and buff and work to bring out the grain and reveal the richness that was in the wood just waiting to shine forth.

Now when I look at that burnished and beautiful chest, I sometimes think of how much we are all like "naked" furniture. We might not like to see what's under our paint or veneer. We might be shocked at how bare of beauty it is. If we're honest enough to look at the nicks and notches, we might just cover them up. We might not be willing to do all the rubbing and buffing needed to let our true beauty shine forth!

..*.*.*.*

Dear Lord, you and I know it's time for a fix-it-yourself project. It's a project that will take a lot of sweat, tears, and exasperation—a project that will never be really finished—and the object of the project is ME. My family and friends are sometimes too willing to point out my nicks and notches but, Lord, you and I know that I'm the one who will have to add the finishing touches to bring out the richness you gave me. Thank you, Lord, for all the possibilities—but don't be surprised if I come crying to you for help when the paint starts oozing and the stripping starts dripping!

32 I'm Being Followed

I suspect I'm under suspicion. There must be a secret agent reading my secret grocery list or peeking in my kitchen window.

Major manufacturers must have hired industrial spies to follow me every time I go shopping. The minute they notice that I have found a product I like, they send a message by satellite to their main office advising them to stop production on that item immediately.

Sometimes, just to keep me guessing, instead of dropping the product, they "improve" it until it no longer tastes right, looks right, or works right. Does this happen to you, too? Or am I the only one in America who has been targeted by spies?

Once I found a lipstick color I really liked and I used it for a long time. Then one day I bought a fresh tube that looked the same and was labeled the same but when I put it on, it was a brand new color. I got mad and wrote the company to complain. Instead of an apology, they sent me three new tubes of the color I didn't like!

Once I found a flavored rice that I liked so much I used it in a recipe that won a prize in a cooking contest. As soon as the spies noted this, they took it off the market and I could never again make my prize-winning recipe.

Well, maybe I shouldn't be too surprised. As soon as I learned to speak fluent baby talk and adjusted to spending days in the sandbox or baby pool, making peanut butter sandwiches, passing out cookies and mopping up spills of perma-dye Cool-Drink, I looked around and every kid in sight was going off to school.

Just when I started settling into the role of grammar-school room mother, bouncing around on school buses on field trips, dodging hurtling small bodies and large balls while acting as "guard" on the school playground, and making "cute" favors for school parties, I looked around and every kid in sight was taller than I was and talking about high school.

Will I ever get ahead of this game of life? Will I ever learn new songs before they become old? Will I ever wear the right hemline before a newer one becomes fashionable? Will I ever read the books on the best-seller list before they become out-of-print titles?

And will those spies ever quit following me?

· ₊ * · ₊ * · ₊ *

Dear Lord, am I a square in a round world? Have I been trying to set a straight course when life is a series of cloverleafs? Have I kept trying to hang onto the past instead of charging forth with glee and grit to welcome tomorrow? Remind me, Lord, to appreciate the fact that it's more fun to look into an ever-changing, multi-colored, multi-faceted kaleidoscope— instead of staring at a pretty but unchanging scene through rose-colored glasses. Remind me, Lord, that your world is always changing and evolving and growing. Teach me how to "transition"—and to enjoy it.

But, Lord, if you happen to know a store that still has my favorite lipstick or rice, could you sorta make my car turn into their parking lot some day? I would be ETERNALLY grateful!

33 The Muddle-Aged Mutant Unhinged Turtle

This week, as I went to the neighborhood swimming pool for a quick dip, I finally figured out the secret reason that life today is so "weighty." It's because we have all become turtles!

I don't mean slow like turtles. Some of us move so swiftly we move ourselves right into heart attacks, stress attacks, crackups, breakdowns, and the heartbreak of bitten fingernails.

The reason we're turtle-like is because we take our "house" with us wherever we go. But I didn't realize this until that trip to the pool.

Since I was going swimming, I naturally took along a swimsuit, towel, thongs, and my ridiculous-looking noseclip. But then—just in case—I also took suntan lotion, moisturizer, sunglasses, sun visor, a book and a newspaper (just in case there was no one there to visit with), an apple (just in case I got hungry), my coin purse (just in case I got thirsty for a diet cola from the soft-drink machine), and my driver's license (just in case I got stopped by a policeman while driving the six blocks to the pool).

As I was dragging all this stuff along with me from the car, a little boy arrived to swim. He was walking along, barefoot, wearing his swimsuit and carrying a towel—period. That was it. That's all he needed to enjoy his dip. I looked at all my appurtenances and realized I had become a turtle.

Then I began to think about how often we do this. When we go on vacation, we take half the house with us. If there's anything we might need—just in case—we don't leave home without it. Even when we go on a picnic, a camping trip, or a weekend outing "to get away from it all," we can't get away because we take it all with us!

Maybe that's why our society has become anxious, overburdened, troubled, and insecure. Maybe our turtle-like ways are robbing us of God's special gift of time. Maybe we have so many things to worry about and care for that there's no time left to smell the flowers, hear the music, and soar with the eagles. Maybe we've become muddle-aged mutant unhinged turtles!

Dear Lord, forgive my turtle ways. I know that turtles must be anxious and insecure because they are always darting their heads back inside their shells to hide. And they must be overburdened, carrying those heavy houses around all the time. I don't know if there are "troubled" turtles because of another one of their problems—they don't communicate too well.

No wonder I can identify with them. All this "carrying" I do has made my neck muscles tense and my shoulders sag. I communicate often but not always well. Help me, Lord, to stop hurrying and scurrying, to come out of my shell and look up and out instead of always in. Help me to change from a turtle to a turtledove. And the next time I decide to get away from it all, remind me to leave my house at home!

34 Thanks for the Memories

I love to laugh. I love to go to funny movies and hear funny jokes and look at funny pictures. Maybe that's why I love my ancestors. The pictures of them in my family album are the funniest pictures I've ever seen!

There's Uncle Pink and Uncle Ransom and Uncle Grover Cleveland McCarver—and those are their real names, honest! There's Aunt Oskie in her ostrich-feather hat, Grandma in the coat with the big bearskin collar, and solemn, bug-eyed Great-Grandma, who looks like someone just told her that her green tomato pickles did NOT win first prize at the county fair.

I got out the old album the other day after I read an article by a clinical psychologist who said that the "body language" in old photos could tell you a lot about your family. According to the learned doctor, there are a lot of hidden messages in those old faded faces. You're supposed to look and see who's standing next to whom, who's smiling at whom, who looks mad, who looks left out, and who's hiding behind a bush.

The psychologist thinks if you never see a husband and wife pictured together maybe that's because they're trying to pretend they don't know each other. Personally, I think it's just because somebody has to take the picture and they don't want to trust that expensive camera to one of the kids. But maybe that's why he's a famous psychologist and I'm hiding behind a bush.

Whatever those old photos say to you, looking at them is sure a fun way to spend a rainy afternoon. I love to look at Daddy standing on the boardwalk at Atlantic City. He's wearing a three-piece suit and a Panama hat while everybody in the background is in bathing suits! And there's my young and beautiful mother posing coyly under a Chinese paper parasol and my adorable nephew, at age five, sitting on a mule and grinning through a faceful of dirt. And in every single shot since her baby picture, my sister has the same sweet smile that she still wears today. The fashions in the photos change, but not her smile.

They say photographs are one of the first things people try to save when there's a fire in the home. And no wonder. They are irreplaceable reminders of family history, special ceremonies, and the people, places, and milestones of life. That's why looking at them can open a window to yesterday that gives us glimpses of values and hopes and dreams—a solid foundation on which to build the future. And a lot of laughs.

Dear Lord, it's easy to make fun of "the way things used to be" instead of appreciating the lessons that can be learned there. It's easy to blame the mistakes we make today on the way we were treated or taught or spoiled or neglected in the past. Help me, Lord, to learn from—and forgive—the past. Help me to sort through and throw out the trash but save the treasure. And thank you, Lord, for Uncle Pink and Aunt Oskie, for Great-Grandma's frown and my sister's sweet smile. Thank you for yesterday and today.

35 Of Bags and Baggage

He who steals my purse steals trash. But it's trash I can't live without!

It doesn't make sense, I know, but woman has this built-in unquenchable desire to have some kind of bag hanging from her arm. I bet if you could find an actual photograph of Eve, she would be clutching a leaf purse with a grapevine handle. She may not have had any clothes, but you can bet she had a purse!

Wherever you go—grocery store, ballgame, dance, movie, fire sale, or hayride—you'll see all the women there clutching purses. If you see one without a purse, she is probably wringing her hands because she doesn't know what to do with them when they are purse-less.

Just the other day I saw a photograph of Queen Elizabeth at some royal function. She was wearing a jeweled evening gown and a diamond tiara but hanging from a dangling chain over her white-gloved arm was this purse big enough to hold the Magna Carta. It didn't go with the outfit but I'm sure it made her feel secure.

The next day I saw a lady in a leather lumberjack-type jacket, heavy slacks, and boondocker shoes but dangling from her leather-gloved hand was a dainty lady-like purse. Again, it didn't go with the outfit but she looked very secure. Who can explain it? Who can tell me why? Fools give you reasons, wise men never try!

A woman's purse is her survival kit, security blanket, and badge of authority all rolled into one. So how do men manage without one?

I think it's because whenever they need anything, they turn

to a woman and say, "Look in your purse and see if you have some fishing twine. How about a screwdriver? Is there a Band-Aid in there? Do you have the phone number of the auto repair shop, the hardware store, and the Burger Barn?" And, of course, she does. I suspect men don't carry purses because they don't have to!

Dear Lord, I've noticed that with or without a purse, most of us carry around some excess baggage. We should leave this kind of baggage in the will-call and then lose the claim ticket: Fear. Guilt. Doubt. Worry.

I am starting right now to clean out my purse—but I know it won't be as easy to clean out all that other stuff. Help me, Lord, to get rid of fears from the past and stop laying claim to them. Help me to give up guilt and trust in your forgiveness. Help me to pitch out doubt and worry. And Lord, please help me get this gumdrop loose that is stuck to the lining of my purse!

36 New and Improved?

My house is full of sows' ears. My trash is stuffed with silk purses. And I bet you have the same problem.

It has always been the American way to want to improve everything—to try to make silk purses out of sows' ears.

Politicians are always begging for votes by promising to take the sow by the ear and give us a "change" in government. Parents are always struggling to give their children a "better" life than they've had themselves. And half the products in any store have the same magic words on their labels—"new and improved."

But recently I've noticed something scary. We seem to have stopped trying to improve the product and are only interested in improving the PACKAGE. I go to the store and buy the same old something I've been buying for years—but now it's packaged in six layers of plastic, attached to a flower-decorated piece of cardboard, costing twice as much as before. It takes a pair of scissors, a kitchen knife, and two broken fingernails to get it open—then I throw the silk-purse packaging into the trash and put the same old sow's ear on my shelf.

When we get the same old product but are told it's new and improved because of its packaging, we are given the message that only the packaging is important, that it's what's outside that counts—not what's inside.

The same is true of TV programming. If the show is packaged with a beautiful star, fancy settings, and a laugh track, who complains about the fact that all the characters are totally immoral, all the situations make fun of traditional values, and all the lines are just a little dirty?

And that, of course, brings us to today's people. If they're "packaged" correctly—in expensive clothes, with important friends, a fancy car, and a "good" address—do we care if they have interior spirituality, morals, or values? If they look young and "with it," do we think that's more important than the wisdom of maturity? If they have a stylish hairdo on the outside of the head, do we let that influence us more than what's going on inside the head?

Have we accepted non-Christian lifestyles packaged as progress, unfaithfulness packaged as liberation, and disobedience to God's laws packaged as intellectual freedom? Have we been sold what looks like a silk purse only to find ourselves stuck with a sow's ear?

Dear Lord, help me to remember that YOU are the true packaging expert. You made the eggshell—that perfect, protective container that is so easy-to-open when it's time to spill out its precious contents.

You made the clouds that look fragile, yet are sturdy enough to collect and hold drops of water until it's time to pour them down as refreshing rain.

You made the tulip bulb that lies buried through the cold, dark winter, and then bursts forth with beautiful spring blossoms. And you made that amazing package of skin and bones that holds each human being.

Help me, Lord, to be discerning, to look beyond the world's kind of packaging—both of people AND ideas. And thank you, Lord, for YOUR packaging—and all the wonderful "surprise" packages you've sent me. Sometimes your "wrappings" are puzzling, but once I look inside, your gifts are wondrous to behold!

37 Feathering the Nest with Dad

Today's dads could learn a thing or two from the male Emperor Penguin. He's a real bird of a father!

It seems that all the mother penguin does is lay one single egg and her job is finished. Then she flies away from home, abandoning the nest—except she hasn't even bothered to do any home-building so there IS no nest. She just takes off and leaves the old man standing out in the cold.

The father Emperor Penguin hatches the offspring by standing upright and holding the egg ON TOP OF HIS FEET for two months!

Do you realize what that means? No fly-by-nights out with the boys, no bowling or golf or baseball—and no food! Once Mom decides she deserves a break today and leaves, she doesn't even fly by with a bag of burgers until after the chick is hatched. Now there is a liberated mother. AND a dedicated father.

Meanwhile, back in the human kingdom, the feat of fathering is going through some dramatic changes. Role models are shifting and more fathers are helping with housework and cooking and child care (at least that's what I read in the papers—although I don't see a lot of it in my immediate neighborhood!).

But as mothers are finally getting a better "image" and being recognized and respected for their qualities and equality, the image of fathers may be suffering. There was a time when a father was depicted as a tower of strength, the breadwinner, the provider, the strong arm to lean on, the protector, the honorable man.

Only occasionally would there be an exception—like the cartoon of Dagwood Bumstead. He was the well-meaning but absent-minded goof-off, the forgetful sleepyhead. And people laughed because he was not really typical—not really the image most people had of a father.

Unfortunately, today it seems fathers are USUALLY depicted as the bumbler—in commercials, movies, and TV programs. Today, fathers just "don't get no respect."

Maybe in the past we expected too much of dads, expecting them to be always in charge, the leader, the one responsible for guidance and discipline, and the very bread of life. Or maybe we asked too little, leaving them on the sidelines when it came to nurturing.

Maybe we should all take a more realistic look at the role of fatherhood and the role we ALL play in either ridiculing it or honoring it. Maybe we've been leaving fathers out in the cold like that poor Emperor Penguin!

..*.*.*.*

Dear Lord, help me to be less ready to ridicule and more eager to honor those who deserve it. Remind me that we all have different roles to play, each as important as the other—AND as difficult. Thank you, Lord, for all the fathers who have come into my life at different times and made it more comfortable, more interesting, and more fun—my own father, grandfather, and husband, plus fathers who have been neighbors, business acquaintances, or good friends. Help them all, Lord. And help the rest of us to be more concerned with their feelings and give them more respect!

38 Don't Tell Alexander Graham Bell

My husband spends as little time as possible on the telephone. He thinks three or four sentences should be adequate for anyone to get any message across to anyone else. And then it's time to hang up.

Evidently he managed to program himself to use the phone for business purposes but he could never understand anyone voluntarily choosing to use it for social chit-chat. Maybe that's why it seems to be totally beyond the realm of possibility for him to take telephone messages for me.

For example, we were sitting quietly watching the news on TV one evening when a newsman named John appeared on the screen. This seemed to trigger a distant spot in my husband's memory bank. He said, "That reminds me. Someone named Joan called you last week." I said, "Joan? Joan who?"

He thought for a minute and then responded, "Maybe it wasn't Joan. It might have been Jean or June or Jan. Anyway, she wanted you to call her back right away."

Right away? I could lose a lot of friends like that!

Another time, the message came only a day late—but it was a bit garbled. My husband suddenly said, "Oh, by the way, some missionary called you yesterday."

Missionary? What kind of missionary? And why was he calling? My husband couldn't remember any further details or whether there had been a message. I spent a couple of days wondering who I knew who might have an urgent message for me from some far-flung mission outpost. Then I received a call from a local store.

They said they had called me earlier to tell me the

"Franciscan Ware" dishes I ordered had come in; they were wondering why I hadn't come in to pick them up. Missionary indeed!

Dear Lord, I know that I, too, should be more careful to pay attention to what others are trying to tell me. I know I have sometimes been guilty of half-listening, interrupting in the middle of a sentence, daydreaming, or thinking of what I want to say next instead of really concentrating on what the other person is saying.

In my dealings with others, Lord, help me to try to understand THEIR side of the story before I begin to present mine. Help me to give my undivided attention, listening to others—and to you. And, Lord, could you please appear to my husband in a vision and tell him to start WRITING DOWN my phone messages?

39 Just a Taste

There is no accounting for some people's tastes! That's one of the basic facts I learned at my mother's knee. But I didn't know the same was true with animals until we got a dog who ate green apples and ice cubes.

That dog was always so close on the heels of my son and his friends that he thought he was "one of the boys." Naturally, he ate what they ate. When I handed out green apples, he expected one too. And when he saw the boys bite into theirs, he settled down to gnaw dutifully, just like his buddies.

In the summer, when I ran out of popsicles, the boys had to settle for ice cubes, and the dog learned to beg for those too. In fact, if I had ever entered that dog in a competition, the one medal he could have won would have been "pedigreed beggar"!

The worst was the first time I opened a can of chili after the dog had come to live at our house. The minute that aroma hit the air, the dog came to attention, looking longingly at the stove and giving me the poor-pitiful-hungry-little-me look. Up until that moment, I had had no reason to suspect that my dog had Mexican ancestry.

When I sat down to eat the chili, his eyes followed every spoonful I lifted. Before long, we were both in a terrible emotional state. He was shaking and whimpering so much that I was afraid he was going to start a Mexican hat dance! Finally, I decided to put a spoonful of chili into his bowl, sure that the first fiery bite would discourage him. I was wrong. He loved the taste so much, he gave new meaning to the phrase, "Give it a lickin'."

A few days later, I opened a carton of raspberry yogurt.

Suddenly, the dog's gourmet nose went into action again. Since yogurt does not exactly smell like chili, I thought his nose had misfired. To show him he had made a mistake, I put a spoonful of yogurt into his dish. He lapped up every drop.

Well, I suppose it was inevitable that our dog have strange tastes. Everybody else in the family does. My son likes fried okra. When I serve that, my husband acts like we're trying to poison him if we even let the bowl of okra come near his end of the table. But my husband likes cornmeal mush and puts pepper on sweet potatoes. And I am the one who indulgently puts up with my husband, my son, and the dog. There is just no accounting for some people's tastes!

Dear Lord, you must have had a lot of fun making animals—and people—with such different tastes! Some of my casual acquaintances will rush in the front door and give me a big hug. Some lifelong friends act like a handshake is an invasion of privacy. Some people will go to church and sing out loud, sing out strong—whether they know how to sing or not. Others will never warble a note. And let's not even think about the differences people have when you start talking about art or politics or the best spaghetti recipe.

Lord, thank you for putting so many strange tastes in your world. It just wouldn't have been as delicious without all the differences!

40 It's a Mystery!

"Who done it?" is a popular phrase at our house—and not just when a dish gets broken or a secret gets spilled.

My husband started it—like he starts lots of things! He is a long-time mystery fan. His favorite music is the soundtrack from that old movie, "How To Murder Your Wife." (I hope it's just the music he likes and not the plot!)

When we were first married, I couldn't understand why he wasted his time reading junky mysteries. Then I landed in the hospital for a few days and, instead of bringing me flowers or candy, my beloved brought me a paperback murder mystery. When I opened the package, I wanted to murder HIM.

But being the wonderful person that I am—and having absolutely nothing else to do—I read the book. It was the best medicine he could have brought me! I didn't have time to think about aches, pains, or the hospital heebie-jeebies. I was too busy reading as fast as I could, trying to figure out "who done it."

After that, I understood and shared my husband's mysterious reading habit. Now we both can enjoy mystery books, movies, and TV shows.

Maybe we like them so much because when we were growing up, there wasn't much mystery in our lives. His youth was pretty much like mine. My parents watched every move I made, told me what to do and not to do, where I could go, and where I couldn't go and exactly what time I was expected to get home. I hated it.

They also let me know they loved me and complimented me when I did anything right and bragged about me to their friends. I hated that too. I was embarrassed to overhear them talking about me.

Maybe because of their protective smothering, I was a late bloomer. It took me a while to grow up. And I've been grateful ever since. I've enjoyed being an independent adult, but I'm glad I didn't miss that time when I was a protected, loved child.

Dear Lord, today's psychology tells us parents to leave the kids alone, let them make their own decisions, do their own thing. We parents are supposed to be free to live our own lives instead of spending so much time caring for or helping our children. I'm sure all this must be very wise and right for some—but I'm grateful my parents never heard about it!

Lord, help today's parents know how to "hold tight with open hands." Help us to teach our children that freedom must be balanced by some basic rules and commandments. Help us to show them that loving dependence can take some of the fear out of independence. And help us to find the time to ENJOY sharing those youthful years. All too soon, babies grow into independent adults, and parents wonder where the years and the opportunities went. It's a mystery!

41 Throwing a Temperature Tantrum

Some people blow hot and cold. I know. I'm one of them. Like Goldilocks tasting the porridge, I test the temperature and usually find it "too hot" or "too cold." I never seem to feel "just right." Instead, I'm either burning up or freezing. My husband says my thermostat must be broken.

His temperature is always the same. Some like it hot. He likes it cold. But even more than cold, he likes "fresh air." All year he's opening windows to "air out the house"—summer, winter, rain, snow, or whatever. As a result, our house is sometimes a sauna and often a refrigerator. Since my broken thermostat can't adjust to that, I've become a quick-change artist.

In the summer, with windows open, I've got on shorts and a blouse, dashing about doing chores. Then, just when I've worked up a lather, my husband starts closing windows. On comes the air conditioner and gusts of frigid air pour onto my sweltering brow. It's time to change into slacks and sweater.

But when house chores are finished, there's yard work to do and that means changing back to the shorts, since you can't garden while dressed like Nanook of the North. By the time I've conquered the great outdoors, it's time to head for the grocery store—but that's air-conditioned, so it's time to change again.

When I put on my high-necked, long-sleeved grocery store clothes, they're too hot to be comfortable "in transit." The obvious solution is the automobile's air conditioning but my husband warns me that my old car's old air conditioner is bad for the old car's old motor. He suggests that instead of using it, I should open all the car windows because I will ENJOY all that nice, fresh air.

You can see that, at all times, I am in danger of having a temperature tantrum!

Dear Lord, at least I get a lot of exercise running back and forth to the closet. Maybe I should be grateful for that. And besides, I've noticed that I'm not the only quick-change artist who blows hot and cold. Politicians constantly change campaign promises. Corporate executives suddenly change the rules of the game and the office. Kids can be angels one minute and not the next. Help us all, Lord, and forgive our quick changes. As we wander and wonder, changing, learning, seeking guidance, show us the way. Remind us to pray more so that, some day, we will stop blowing hot and cold and learn how to live "just right."

42 Put a Cork in It!

I've always known my husband was a corker, but this week he proved it. He announced he would like my help in corking a wall. That sounded like a good idea, so I agreed.

It was NOT a good idea.

You see, the only way to apply this cork to a wall is with an awful, tar-like substance that's a lifetime glue. It's so thick you have to use a trowel to dig it out of the can. Then you sort of hurl this black stuff toward the wall and try to smear it around quickly without spilling any on anything.

I spilled it on everything. From that moment on, we were stuck with each other. We had glue stuck on our clothes, in our hair, on our hands and in our shoes. We were not a pretty sight.

Oh well, it might not have been a fun experience, but it sure was an exciting one—all that shouting at each other, words and glue flying through the air, cork and insults being flung about, hammers and harangues dropped, tacks and tempers lost.

And it was well worth the trouble when we ended up with this bright, spanking new, cork-covered wall—interestingly decorated here and there with big black smudges of leftover glue. Luckily, my husband had plans for that wall and has already covered the whole thing with pinned-on maps. Now only we, the perpetrators, know about the dark smudges that lie hidden—like so many family secrets—beneath the bright cork veneer seen by outsiders.

· ★ · ★ · ★ · ★

Dear Lord, I guess most families have some smudges like that, known only to a select few. Whenever you start digging up a family tree or paging through the past, you usually find a few black marks, a shady story here, a dark whisper of doubt there. But, Lord, I know that doesn't excuse it or make it right. Every time I pass that wall, I feel a twinge of guilt.

Maybe we could have done better. Maybe we should have planned ahead—or something drastic like that. And certainly, we could have given our vocal chords less exercise. Forgive us our tempers, Lord. But at least we learned a valuable lesson. Some people can design skyscrapers or build space rockets. We can't. Some people can wallpaper and lay carpet and cork walls. We can't. We've learned, Lord, that it's important to recognize our own limitations. Please, Lord, don't let us ever even think about corking a wall again!

43 Anyone for Tea?

Ahhhfternoon teatime... fine china, silver, crumpets, and cake... "one lump or two?" How veddy sophisticated and elegant.

Although sophistication is not exactly my cup of tea, I got all excited when I saw a newspaper ad announcing that "High Tea" was now being served every afternoon at one of our fanciest downtown hotels. My friend Mary's birthday was approaching, and this seemed like a jolly good way to celebrate.

So Mary and I got all gussied up and headed downtown. As we pulled into the front driveway of the hotel, I slowed to look for a parking spot but, before I had time to think about it, a hotel attendant approached, offering to park the car for me. As I handed him my car keys—with pinkie finger extended—I was feeling rather regal, visions of sugarplums and teacups dancing in my head. We toddled off to tea.

It was even "veddy much nicer" than we had expected—specially blended tea, tiny finger sandwiches, lovely little cakes, and chocolate-dipped strawberries. And they even brought Mary a yellow rose for her birthday while the person tickling the ivories on the Baby Grand piano played an appropriately demure "Happy Birthday to You."

We sipped and chewed as slowly as possible, stretching out the treat as long as we could, but finally it was time to return to the real world. We must have emerged from the hotel at check-out, check-in time because we stepped into a whirl of very fancy activity—a white-gloved doorman welcoming guests who had just arrived in a looong stretch-limo, a swanky black import car waiting for its driver, cabs darting in and out, picking up or letting out people who were dressed as if they went to High Tea every day.

Suddenly it dawned on me that at any moment, this world of affluence was going to be jarred by an attendant driving my old rust bucket—my ancient vehicle that's now trimmed with a lacy fringe of rust along the underside and a designer decoration of jagged rust-outs on each front fender. We scurried to get into the car as fast as possible, to remove our rustiness before we besmirched the beautiful-people picture.

Oh well, it was fun while it lasted. And besides, it was nice to get home, kick off the high heels and snuggle back into my little nest. It's good to fly high occasionally but there's no place like home—even if it has a mortgage and rust spots.

Dear Lord, I know that poor is not necessarily better than rich. I once read a quote that went something like this: "Pharmacists handle many kinds of poisons every day, yet they do not get poisoned themselves because they keep the poisons in their shops, not in their bodies. In the same way, you may possess riches without being poisoned by them—IF you keep them in your house or purse but not in your heart."

So I know, Lord, that wealthy is as wealthy does. Thank you for my snug little nest and the delicious High Tea. But, Lord, help me to remember that wealth, like beauty, is only skin deep and finger sandwiches are just plain old ham-on-white... without the upper crust.

44 The Treasured Dowry

The strangest thing happened today. Out of nowhere, I began thinking about my "former life"—those single, carefree days when I moved into my first apartment. It was a second-floor walkup in an old but charming building. My one window overlooked a tiny garden and there were shining hardwood floors and solid sound-proof walls built to endure.

Luckily, it was furnished, since all I had to bring to it were some clothes, an old typewriter, one set of new sheets, and one pillow. On my first day off from work, I hurried to a small neighborhood store to buy some luxurious apartment additions—cheap pots, pans, and dishes.

For some strange reason, the only plates in that store had scalloped edges and there were holes in the scallops so you could run ribbon through them. Obviously, those plates were meant for a wall, not a table, but I was desperate so I bought two of them.

I couldn't wait to have my first company dinner; I invited the girl who lived across the hall to join me that very night. We had just met so she didn't know any better and accepted the invitation.

Since I didn't know how to cook ANYTHING, spaghetti seemed the easiest thing to try. It may have been easy to cook but we soon discovered that spaghetti was not easy to eat when you had plates with holes on the edges. Instead of ribbon running through them, spaghetti and sauce kept running through. It was an almost-inedible, incredibly giggly meal and I'll never forget it.

Soon I added another luxurious kitchen addition: a hand-held toaster. On one of my bargain-seeking expeditions, I found this strange little wire grill in which you encased one piece of bread. You were supposed to hold the grill over an open gas flame until the bread scorched and then turn it over to scorch the other side.

I think I may have been one of the few persons in history ever to own such an item. It was a wonderful conversation piece and also provided me with some very unusual breakfasts.

As I continued trying to upgrade my standard of living to the level of minimum, I added a well-used easy chair (so well-used, it was over easy!), an old trunk I pretended was a coffee table, and a bookcase that had been trashed by its former owner. By the time I met Prince Charming, I had a dowry full of such treasures.

We continued using some of my dowry items for years but my husband never did warm up to that open-flame toaster. My mother took pity on him and gave us an electric toaster which served us well for years until I was lured by a shiny new toaster on sale and decided to upgrade our standard of living once again.

It was a mistake. The new one is already rejecting rye and tossing wheat and white across the table. They just don't make things like they used to—in my "former life."

* * * * *

Dear Lord, shiny and new is nice but not always better. I've noticed that toasters are not the only things that don't last as long any more. Christmas toys were once so durable, they could be handed down to the next generation. Now they seldom last until the next Christmas! Once friendships lasted a lifetime, families were always together for holidays and Sunday dinners. Now everybody keeps moving away—out of town, out of touch. Help us, Lord, to hold tight to our old tried and true morals and values in these changing times.

Lord, I know that YOU still make things like you used to—babies with little pink toes, sunsets, rainbows, and flowers that bloom in the spring, tra la. Thank you, Lord, thank you.

45 The Games of Life

Did you hear about the lady who called the local game warden to ask for help? She was having a birthday party for her preschooler and hoped the "game" warden could suggest some games to play!

I could have used a game warden at some of my son's birthday parties. I didn't need suggestions. I needed help in rounding up those little "wild animals" who played spontaneous games like "ring around the cake and stick your finger in the icing," "pour the punch on the cat," and "pin the tail on the doggie."

His parties celebrated the fact that he was, of course, one year older. By the end of the day, his mother looked and felt ten years older!

There was the year we had the garage party. I had spent so much time at garage sales that I felt perfectly comfortable inviting company into the garage—especially the kind of company my son kept. They were about eight years old and skilled in spills, chases, stumbling, dropping, and breaking—the perfect group to keep in a garage. At the end of the party, it was so much easier to sweep out the trash and the leftover guests.

Then there was the memorable Monster Birthday. Instead of Christmas in July, we had Halloween in May, with ghoulish decorations, red vampire punch, and tombstone place cards. At one of those garage sales, we had found a dressmaker's dummy which we dressed and then splashed the neck with red paint "blood" to make a headless victim to stand in the corner. I gave the kids some of my old cosmetics plus black jellybeans for dragon's teeth and let them make up their faces like monsters. The kids loved it all but their moms were not happy when the little monsters came home with stuff on their faces that was not easy to wash off.

Another year my son was "into" space and asked me to make a cake that looked like a space ship to bring in to his school classroom. At first, this seemed like an impossible dream, but then I realized I could just make a sheet cake, cut off the two front corners to make a "nose cone" and put the cut-off triangles at the other end to look like the "tail section." With a lot of red, white and blue icing, it might resemble a rocket, if not a space ship.

When I staggered into his room carrying the two-foot-long rocket cake, the whole class oohed and aahed. But the big surprise was still to come. I asked the teacher if we could turn off the lights and told the kids to step way back to the other end of the room and "count down" so the rocket could blast off. They giggled and counted. When they shouted, "Blast Off!" I struck a match to the little can of Sterno I had put in the tail section. A bright flame shot up, giving the kids a thrill—and the teacher a stress attack! (Actually, it was safe because I had "practiced" the blastoff at home and knew just how fast I had to slap the lid on the flame.)

I sometimes felt a little jealous when my friends with daughters had fancy, frilly parties with pink and white cakes, bouquets, and balloons—while I was stuck with rockets, vampires, and rampaging rowdies. But I sure had a lot of fun!

*****

Dear Lord, thank you for all those wild and crazy memories. Other kids probably got gifts and parties that cost more money, but I wonder if any were as INTERESTING! And, Lord, I've been thinking that maybe some year I'll go ahead and have a pink-and-white birthday party for my son, complete with flowers, crystal goblets, and finger sandwiches—but I won't invite him or his friends! Do you think that would be proper? I'll just invite MY friends—and you, Lord—and we'll have another interesting memory!

46 It Was a Cat-astrophe!

E verywhere I look at our house these days, I spot little golden blobs. No, it's not money. It's blobs of yellow cat fur. I am beginning to suspect that my cat has read the story about kids leaving a trail of bread crumbs to find the way home. Ever since the weather got warm, he has been leaving a trail of fur wherever he goes—so now ANYBODY could find the way home to my house.

Maybe leopards can't change their spots or tigers their stripes but this cat has sure been changing his coat. Actually, I guess it's natural for someone who's been wearing a fat yellow fur coat all winter to feel the need to shed it for the summer. I just wish he wouldn't shed it on my good slacks.

Actually, I'm glad there's a change-of-weather explanation for his change of fur. Otherwise, I might be tempted to take him to a cat psychologist to find out why he's acting this way.

The other day I read about a lady who had to consult a pet psychologist to find out why her usually well-behaved pet was misbehaving. The doctor told her it was because she wasn't spending enough "quality time" with the pet. Expert or no, when I have any quality time to spend, it's not going to be spent with the cat!

Today the idea of "quality time" has become a catch-word, a cure-all for many problems. Some husbands and wives, parents and children think they can be too busy for each other most of the time—and then make up for their apartness by occasionally spending an hour of "quality time" together.

Our world has become work-weary, too busy to just BE.

If we're too busy to find time for each other, then we're surely too busy to find time for prayer. The other day I went to a seminar where it was suggested you should find two twenty-minute times each day to just sit quietly and put yourself in the presence of God. Many in the audience (including me) began to wonder how they could find those two pieces of time to set aside in each busy day. Yet those same people (including me) find SEVERAL twenty-minute segments each day to fret, fume, criticize—or clean up cat fur.

Maybe we've been forgetting how important it is to leave a trail of prayer, thoughtfulness, and togetherness—so we can find our way home.

Dear Lord, here I am saying I'm sorry again. But I am. I know I should spend more time in quiet prayer. But you must admit I DO spend a lot of time in loud conversation with you. Thank you for listening, Lord. Stay with me, and help me to make it through every busy day so that I won't just leave a trail of crumbs but a trail of something more substantial, more lasting, more loving. And, Lord, could you PLEASE help that cat get rid of his coat so he and I both can stop worrying about the de-furring and get back to our purring!

47 Who's in the Driver's Seat?

If you are judged by the car you keep, I am in a no-parking zone on the highway of life. A friend once gave me the perfect description of my car: "The inside of your car is such a jumble, it looks like a purse on wheels!"

Yep, that's my car—a purse on wheels.

My husband is afraid to ride in my car—not because he thinks I'm an unsafe driver but because he's afraid he won't be able to find a seat. Some friends LIKE to ride with me because their cars look the same, and seeing mine makes them feel less guilty.

Actually, I'm not really messy, just "prepared." One snowy day, I looked into the back seat. There were snow boots, an umbrella, a hat, gloves, coat hanger, a small American flag, and a book. I rationalized that, in case of emergency, I could always wave the flag to attract attention, or I could just sit and read the book until help arrived. If help did not arrive, I could put on my warm hat, gloves, and boots, and, taking my umbrella and coat hanger for protection, I could wade through the snow to get help!

My rationalization became prophetic. Two days later, the emergency arrived. As I was hurtling along in the fast lane as usual, my car got tired. It turned off its motor to take a nap.

Luckily, I managed to coast almost off the road and my car ended up partly on the shoulder and partly in danger of being smashed to smithereens at any moment by oncoming traffic.

I put on my hat and gloves, since the heater was also taking a nap, but I decided it was snowing too hard for anyone to see me waving the flag. And I couldn't quite relax enough to read the book.

103

Instead, I read the owner's manual that had been in the glove compartment, untouched, for many moons. It had nothing to suggest for a car napping on a snowy shoulder.

I was just about to reach for the boots, umbrella, and coat hanger when a police car came. The officer called a tow truck, which towed me to the nearest little countryside gas station. The local yokels opened the hood, peered in, shook their heads and began to whistle "Taps." Since the tow truck driver was still inside drinking coffee, he agreed to tow me—at great cost—to my friendly neighborhood garage where I am "known." They have seen my pitiful pleading act before, so they agreed to bring my car back to life.

While it was being rehabilitated, I began to realize how dependent I was on this four-wheeled wonder. How did women of generations past manage to raise children, run errands, keep house, and keep their sanity without auto-mation? How did Cleopatra ever set styles on the Nile with only a chauffeur-driven barge? How did Madame Curie ever discover anything when she had to take a horse or a trolley to the laboratory? How did our grandmothers survive without a purse on wheels?

․•*․*•*․*

Dear Lord, every day I hit the highways and byways, list in hand, confident that I know where I'm going and how to get there. But when I hit a detour or have a breakdown, I realize I'm not really in control. Remind me, Lord, not to be too dependent on "things" or routines. I should only be dependent on YOU. Thank you, Lord, for my purse on wheels. Ride with me and help me remember that I am the traveler—but YOU are in the driver's seat!

48 The Lopsidedness of Life

I had a close call in the kitchen today. I almost broke a treasured family tradition by baking a cake that was NOT lopsided!

Sometime in the distant past, my son decided his most favorite dessert in the world was my yellow cake with chocolate-almond icing. Since then, he's always requested that cake for every birthday and special occasion. The invited guests at these occasions could not understand his enthusiasm for this rather everyday dessert, but to him it was always special.

And it has become a family tradition that every time I make this no-frills cake, the finished product turns out lopsided. Either the cake cooks crooked or the cook crooks her finger wrong or whatever—but the top layer always slides off the bottom layer while I frantically try to hold back gravity with a spatula, praying for the frosting to harden fast enough to keep the top glued on.

Today, for no apparent reason, things were different.

When I finished icing the cake, I suddenly realized something was very wrong. It looked just like other people's cakes. It looked almost like a bakery cake. It was NOT lopsided.

I knew my son would be disappointed, but it was too late to do anything about it. In despair, I started washing up the pots and pans, knowing I had failed the family tradition.

But then, out of the corner of my eye, I sensed a movement. Quickly, I checked the cake. Sure enough, the top layer was very slowly sliding sideways! With a great sense of satisfaction—and years of practice—I propped up one side of the cake plate so the top layer would have to stop in mid-slide. Soon the icing hardened and held and I had a perfect lopsided cake ready for my son's traditional birthday celebration!

..*.*.*

Dear Lord, sometimes we expect families to be soooo perfect. But sometimes lopsided is more fun—and certainly more realistic! In fact, the lopsided members of my family are the ones we remember the most. We still chuckle about Aunt Linnie who used to save string and bury silver dollars in her backyard in case paper money became worthless. She was stingy with some things but often very generous to us. Nosy Aunt Ellen could ask twenty-five questions in twenty-four minutes but at least she was interested in us. And Uncle Grover smoked so many cigars, he could sit outside all summer and no mosquito would dare bite him for fear of nicotine poisoning. But he was so kind and gentle, he was my favorite uncle. Thank you, Lord, for all our lopsided relatives.

If I ever get impatient with some of the irritating habits of our kith and kin, help me to remember that even the families in Norman Rockwell's paintings had freckles and lopsided smiles—and that's what made them so interesting. Remind me that sometimes lopsidedness IS the "icing on the cake!"

49 It's a Jungle in Here!

Sometimes I used to wonder what was lurking in the jungle in our family room. Now I know.

When we first moved to this house, I put a few plants in a corner right by the patio door. Those plants grew like weeds until we had a corner jungle. Actually, it's been nice because in the summer, it looks like the outside plants have grown right through the wall into the house. And in the winter, all that greenery holds the promise of springtime to come again.

But plants are like children. They're bright and beautiful and make a room come alive. But they sure can be messy.

Last week—after only 12 years of thinking about it—we finally decided to put some new carpeting in the family room. This meant removing everything from the room—including all those plants. Now I would find out what lurked in the greenery.

All right, I know I should have been cleaning in, under, and around the potted corner every Tuesday or at least every full moon. But it's fun to leave a little mystery in one's life.

Well, now the time had come. Bright and early, before the carpetman was due, I lugged the plants to the patio and hosed them down. They were surprised to be sniffing outside air and getting a real shower. And I was surprised to discover that, underneath it all, the corner was hiding only a few small cobwebs, some fallen leaves and a small springling of spilled potting soil.

But then, while the carpet was being rolled out, the sky darkened. What had started as a steamy, hot summer morning turned into a tropical storm. And if that was not bad enough, it began to hail. The first time my plants had been outside in twelve years and they were being pelted by hailstones!

I could hear them whimpering and whining and calling me

107

ugly botanical names. The hail soon stopped, the sun came back, the carpet got tacked down and the plants moved back inside with their freshly washed faces to snuggle safely into their corner for another twelve years. The hail had caused no damage and they looked even more beautiful than before. But for my home-body houseplants, it had certainly been an exciting morning!

Dear Lord, the experience with my plants is typical of living in today's world. We hear about drive-by shootings, dishonest politicians, disintegrating families, and dysfunctions everywhere we look—we begin to wonder what is lurking in every corner. Sometimes we're even afraid to look into the corners of the minds of our friends or relatives. They might tell us how much they like a recent movie or TV show that is obviously immoral or un-Christian. They might laugh about how they cheated some-one in a business deal. They might look the other way when a commandment is being broken, using the excuse "everyone's doing it today."

Lord, in today's jungle, even the "good" people are all too often confused or misled by distorted media "facts." and, Lord, what is even scarier is the fact that "they" might be "us" or "me." Help me, Lord, to not get lost in the jungle or find some-thing worse than cobwebs lurking in the corner of my own family room. And thank you, Lord, for my new carpet, my sturdy green plants and your evergreen promise that goodness CAN prevail—even over sudden storms and hailstones on a summer day.

50 Innocent until Proven Guilty

It's a good thing I didn't get murdered in my sleep last Tuesday night. If I had, the detectives would surely have pinned it on the wrong person.

You've probably watched one of those mystery movies where the investigator questions a suspect: "Where were you between midnight and 5 A.M.? What was your relationship to the deceased? And why is there a button missing from your raincoat?"

Clues are gathered, and speculation begins. Did the butler do it? Was it the butcher, baker, or candlestick maker? Or was it Great-Aunt Sue? Sometimes the clue that unmasks the guilty party turns out to be something as outlandish as a silvery paper clip in an ashtray or an ash on a silver serving tray. And the minute Chief Inspector Gumshoe spots this clue, the case is solved.

That's why I'm so glad I didn't get murdered Tuesday night. You see, on Wednesday morning, when I made up the bed, I found this little twist-tie next to one of the pillows, the kind of twist you usually find on the opening end of a plastic wrapper that's on the end of a loaf of bread—but not on the end of a bed!

I have no idea what twist of fate put that twist-tie in our bedroom. But, since that's just the kind of clue they always get excited about, the Inspector might have pounced on it—and pointed to a perpetrator who was perfectly innocent. As Gumshoe wrapped up the case, he would have said something like, "Aha! A twist-tie from a bread wrapper! Obviously the murderer is—the baker from the bread store where Great-Aunt Sue bought the sourdough roll she dropped in the collection basket at church last Sunday!"

Well, I'm grateful I found that twist-tie before Inspector Gumshoe did. Now that I think about it, the guilty one who left that twist-tie by my pillow was probably the cat! And it could have been worse—the "murderer" COULD have left a dead mouse!

Dear Lord, I confess. False clues have sometimes led me to punish the innocent, excuse the guilty, and point a finger of blame in the wrong direction. I have punished someone for the "crime" of hurting my feelings or my pride when the accused actually meant no harm or insult and should have been treated as innocent until proven guilty. And all too often, the ones who got punished were my nearest and dearest—family and friends. Forgive me, Lord, for my pointing finger. The next time I am tempted to accuse someone, remind me first to point to myself and ask, "Should you be accusing someone else or could YOU be the guilty one?"

51 Mourning the Morning

One day last week as I was dashing off to an early appointment, I saw a lady coming out her front door to get the morning newspaper. She was wearing fuzzy house slippers, a pink flowered robe, a bright red coat thrown around her shoulders, and a fur hat.

That really made my day. All this time I thought I was the only one who dressed like that in the morning.

On days when I have "business" to conduct, I manage to get up and get dressed properly before leaving the house. But if it's a slow morning and my motor hasn't turned over yet, I am apt to appear in a strange assortment of clothing as I stumble outside to put the mail in the box or the trash in the can before pickup time.

I don't even think about what I'm wearing until I get back in the house and catch sight of myself in a mirror. One cool spring morning, I saw myself wearing a nightgown, raincoat, rain hat, socks, and house shoes. One cold winter morning, I had on a short hooded jacket over a long robe and snow boots.

Maybe such outfits will keep me humble. At least they will help my neighbors open their eyes a little wider in the morning as they start the day thinking, "There, but for the grace of God, go I."

Actually, I guess there are a lot of people like me who sometimes think we are the "only one"—the only one who has a house coming apart at the seams, the only one who hasn't found fame and fortune, the only one who has a sore big toe, the only one who ever does something weird or stupid.

Well, now when I start thinking I am an "only," I will remember that whatever my problem—whether it's a silly little aggravation or a terrible trouble—there are plenty of others who share the same worry. I may not know who they are or where they live but they are there. And they might live right in my own neighborhood.

Knowing that others have problems does not diminish mine, but it is somehow reassuring to know that there are others who are also searching and stumbling—and surviving. I am not alone.

Dear Lord, it's easy to think that I am unique—that I am the only one who is lazy or messy or disorganized or tired. It's easy to think that I am the only nonachiever or the only one who can't make gelatin gel. Thank you, Lord, for showing me that I am never the only one. But, Lord, please remind me to be a little more careful about choosing those one-of-a-kind outfits before I step out the door in the morning.

52 The Frill of It All

When I was at that dangerous teen age, my mother thought if one ruffle looked good, a hundred would make me a social success. She loved to sew and make me wear whatever came out of her machine. As a result, I went frilled and ruffled to ballgames, funerals, scavenger hunts, Halloween parties (the only place my outfit was appropriate), and anywhere else I was invited.

In all the family album snapshots, I am beruffled, beribboned, and usually bedraggled. But during adolescence, I was too bewitched, bothered, and bewildered to protest or even to realize I was suffering from ruffle overload. And, since I knew nothing about psychiatry, I also had no idea that such a frilling experience should be ruining my psyche and giving me an ingrained terror of anything puckered (like those little lines that have appeared around my eyes recently).

On the other extreme, when my son reached the teen emergency zone, he always looked like he had just crawled out of a clothes-for-the-needy donation box. If I was the victim of overdress, he made up for it by sinking to the depths of underdress.

His idea of style was ragged shorts, sloppy shirts, and one pair of shoes he wore EVERYWHERE—from church to overnight cave exploring. He would spend an hour in the shower and then step out to look through a pile of rumpled clothes on the floor to find something bad enough for the outfit of the day.

When it came to our experience of fashion, there was definitely a generation gap. But there were other gaps too.

When I was a teen, our music was loud enough to make our parents complain but not loud enough to cause permanent hearing damage. We worried about not getting invited to the big dance—not about getting mugged, damaging the planet by using up all our natural resources, or nuclear fallout. Since our generations come from two "different worlds," is it any wonder we have difficulty with dialogue, communication, understanding?

But then I guess all generations have suffered from gap-itis and have survived. They say failure is the line of least persistence—so we must keep trying to close the gap and not get too tuckered out by that persistent pucker!

·ₓ*·ₓ*·ₓ*

Dear Lord, maybe it's too bad we parents haven't had the kinds of experiences our children have had—to learn about other cultures, to engage in social action projects, to travel more (either in person or by the TV screen), to communicate by computer. But Lord, maybe it's too bad our children haven't had the experiences we had—of more discipline and safety and innocence. Help us, Lord, to throw away our brooms that try to sweep away each other's likes and opinions. Help us to appreciate each other and to enjoy and learn from our "different worlds." And thank you, Lord, for such a frilling opportunity!

53 If the Shoe Fits...

Last week, I did not put my best foot forward when I went to church.

Running late as usual, I was still shoeless when my husband honked the horn impatiently. I grabbed my black pumps from the closet, stepped into them, and dashed for the car. We were lucky to get a good parking spot so it was just a few steps to the door and it wasn't until the middle of the service that I glanced down and noticed that there was something peculiar about my shoes.

Since I frequently wear black (hoping to look thin but only succeeding in looking funereal), I have two pairs of black pumps. One pair has medium heels and a little bow; the other pair has slightly higher heels and no bow. Last Sunday, I wore one of each.

Once again, I had put my foot into it.

I tried to hide my mismatched shoes by putting one foot behind the other. I tried to concentrate on the sermon but the message got lost somewhere in the embarrassment. I kept thinking that soon it would be time to leave and there I'd go in the uneven heels, hippity-hopping down the aisle—and it wasn't even Easter.

Piously keeping my eyes downcast, I cut my eyes back and forth, trying to sneak a peak to see if anyone was snickering behind a songbook. That's when I noticed the lady across the aisle with her head buried in her hands, deep in prayer, obviously troubled by some problem and seeking help.

Next my eye caught sight of a little boy on the other side. He had taken a seashell out of his pocket and was studying it as though it held a magic secret. Maybe it did. He may have missed some of the sermon (like I did) but he was getting a lasting lesson in the mysteries and wonders of nature.

Just then a baby cooed and laughed and I looked around and saw the young father pick up the baby tenderly, patting its back, smiling at it lovingly. That father's face held a prayer of joy and gratitude.

Too late, I realized that to those people—and to others who were using their time and thoughts WISELY—my mismatched shoes were of little concern. And if there were some who had been looking idly around like I had been, well, maybe they NEEDED a good laugh to help ease a week of life's everyday tensions.

Like so many of my "problems," that absent-minded lapse was only important to ME and, whether or not ANYBODY noticed, it really wouldn't change the course of world history OR church history.

In spite of that lesson learned, instead of stopping to visit outside church, I hippity-hopped out to the car as fast as my mismatched heels would carry me. I didn't mind giving folks one good laugh but I wasn't bold enough to provide an encore.

* * * * * * *

Dear Lord, I hope I will remember those shoes the next time I get worried all out of shape about the fact that my dress is wrinkled all out of shape or my hair is all out of curl or my outfit is all out of style. Who cares what I wear? (as long as it is clean and makes me look ten pounds thinner.) Just kidding, Lord. I will try to worry less about the outside and more about the inside. And when I hear the story about the lilies of the field, I will remember, "If the shoe fits...."

54 Forgotten Treasures— Tut, Tut!

I know just how those explorers felt when they discovered King Tut's tomb. They peered inside and saw treasures—but also strange artifacts that had been buried so long nobody remembered what they once had been. That's how I feel when I look inside my refrigerator.

Whenever I have a case of the hungries, EVERYTHING looks like a treasure—yesterday's leftover spaghetti, the last piece of meatloaf, the few spoonfuls of frozen yogurt in the bottom of the carton. Even the cottage cheese looks good.

But when I start sorting through the little plastic containers and foil-wrapped packages, I sometimes discover strange artifacts buried too long.

Just recently I had a really revolting refrigerator experience.

I had invited friends over to play bridge and had made a fancy cheeseball and some nice snacks. A few minutes before they were due to arrive, a neighbor called asking me to run an urgent errand for her. I dashed out, telling my husband to greet the guests and tell them I would be back soon.

By the time I returned home, my bridge friends knew more about me and my refrigerator than I really wanted them to know.

They had decided to be "helpful" and get out the snacks for me. They had overlooked the fresh cheeseball, the thin-sliced salami, the dip and veggies. They had rummaged around in the back somewhere amid the mystery packages and discovered three small chunks of moldy cheese and a sack of kumquats gone bad!

Now I know that not too many people have good OR bad kumquats in their refrigerator but I had bought some to go around the Christmas turkey because my mother always did that—and then of course I had forgotten them for a month. After all, what do you do with a leftover kumquat?

Dear Lord, today I've been thinking about my refrigerator and King Tut and kumquats and it occurred to me that relationships are like refrigerators. If you leave something on the shelf too long, it goes bad. If you neglect a marriage or a child or a friend or relative, by the time you get back to paying attention, it may be too late. Help me, Lord, to be more alert and attentive. With today's hectic pace, it's easy to forget that you have to keep working on a marriage for it to work. It's easy to get too busy to listen to a child's small problem before it has a chance to grow into a large problem. It's easy to get too involved to find time for a friend or relative. Help me, Lord, to be more careful with my treasures.

55 The Temperamental Toaster

My toaster's been throwing temper tantrums. And do you know why? All of a sudden, it has decided that it hates bagels! Now I realize it might be difficult for a toaster to accept the idea of round bread with a hole in the middle but that is no excuse for this crumby behavior.

I've tried to talk to it. I've cajoled, reasoned, argued, and tried to shame it. I've explained there is more to life than plain sliced bread. But you know how it is. It never listens.

To make matters worse, this truant toaster has started getting violent. When I offer it a bagel, it turns on its red toast-light, examines the foreign object for a few minutes and then activates its reject/eject button. Suddenly, the bagel goes flying across the kitchen counter! Some days, I need a catcher's mitt to field my breakfast.

Obviously, something must be done to correct this dangerous situation. If I let this temperamental toaster get away with insubordination, it could set a bad example for its peer group!

Already the coffee pot is making funny, gurgly noises. Any day now it may begin to reject my favorite brand of coffee—the "sale" brand—and demand a more expensive kind. That could lead to a revolt by the can opener, the blender, or even the microwave. What's a mother to do?

I guess I could abandon bagels and go back to toast. But I have kitchen convictions. No rebellious toaster is going to tell ME what to eat for breakfast—no matter how violent it gets. After all, I'm the boss. I was here first. And besides, I'm bigger than it is!

The only nagging doubt I have about this situation is the

question as to where this toaster picked up the idea that you can hit the reject/eject button any time you encounter something new or different. I might think the toaster had been associating with the "wrong kind," the kind that set a bad example. But the toaster really doesn't get out much. It usually just sits in the same spot in the kitchen where it associates most of the time with— oops—me!

Could I be the bad influence? Do you guess it has noticed ME hit my reject/eject button once too often? Have I been spurning people or ideas that don't instantly fit in with my usual routine? Have I been judging by appearance rather than by content? Am I the one who's been setting a bad example? Uh oh!

Dear Lord, when I was growing up, my mother was always warning me of the danger of setting a bad example. She kept reminding me that if my actions were immoral, uncharitable, unethical, unkind, or uncouth, others might think that ALL your friends acted that way. Of course, she never said anything about influencing toasters! But chasing my breakfast around the kitchen HAS reminded me to be more careful in how I act and react. Help me, Lord, to stop, think—and pray—about new or unfamiliar ideas or people BEFORE I hit that reject/eject button!

56 Wondering about the Seven Wonders

Do you know what the seven wonders of the ancient world were?

I never can remember the whole list but I DO know that they were amazing, awe-inspiring, and almost impossible to imagine.

While I was trying to remember the list, I began making a list of my own—the seven wonders of the modern world. The very first "wonder" on my list would be dirty socks in the hamper INSTEAD of under the bed, behind the sofa, or in a gym bag that has been in the closet long enough to make everything in there smell like something more than a skeleton was buried in that closet.

The second on my list of modern wonders would be this: any line you get in, at the grocery, discount store, etc., that DOESN'T immediately come to a screeching halt because (a) the cash register tape has to be changed, (b) somebody is sorting through coupons, (c) somebody has chosen to buy the one item (out of the 10,467 in that store) that does not have a properly marked or coded price on it.

Third on the list would be any family kitchen that has just been scrubbed, scoured, and shined and can STAY that way—without a dirty dish appearing from nowhere—for at least thirty minutes.

Fourth might be any tot or teen who doesn't continually ask "WHY?"

Fifth would be your favorite commercial TV show WITH-OUT commercials, your favorite teenager's car without dents, or a hot fudge sundae without calories.

Sixth would be another multiple choice: a bathtub that never gets a ring around it, a collar that never gets a ring around it, or a telephone that doesn't wait until your hands are glued together with cookie dough before it gets a ring around it.

Number seven is difficult because there are so many wonders left over, it's hard to settle on the last one. How about a repairman who comes to your house and fixes the problem the FIRST time instead of having to come back and forth (and fifth and sixth)?

Ah yes, seven is definitely not enough wonders for today's world. The eighth wonder would be how we manage to complain so much about everyday aggravations instead of appreciating everyday blessings—and rejoicing in the "wonder" of it all!

Dear Lord, there is one thing I never have to wonder about—your being there when I need you. When I complain, you show me someone who has many more problems than I do. When I grouch, you send me things to make me smile. All day, every day, you are by my side, guiding, teaching, poking me on the shoulder to make me look and see all the wonder-full joys you've put in my path. But, Lord, I DO wish you could do something about those dirty socks!

57 Me and Minnie

Today, I keep thinking about that country music legend, Minnie Pearl. I realize I should be thinking about toxic waste, world peace, or spiritual renewal. But I keep thinking about Minnie—and how she always wore a straw hat with a price tag dangling dizzily from the brim.

Last week, on one of my too-many moments of shopping madness, I just couldn't resist taking home a "darling" straw hat I saw on sale. Then, on Sunday, when Springtime filled the air and Spring Fever filled my head, I decided to really dress up and wear my new hat to church.

When I was all gussied up and ready to sail forth into the world, I admired myself in the bedroom mirror; this was the kind of hat that would turn heads!

Just as I was about to go out the door, I got so carried away with my new look that I picked up a mirror from the dresser and twirled around to see how fabulous my new chapeau looked from the rear. (Normally, I never look into my bedroom rearview mirror because I'm afraid I won't like the view. Besides, my personal philosophy is to look ahead, never back.) But that once, I looked back and saw that—you guessed it—dangling from the darling hat was the sale price tag!

If I hadn't looked back, everybody in church could have gotten a good laugh. As it was, I removed the tag from the hat but couldn't seem to remove the snicker from my face. All through the morning, all I could think of was me and Minnie.

₊₊*₊*₊*

Dear Lord, I think that every time in the next few weeks when I start to feel a little puffed-up and ready to give myself a proud pat on the back, my high-hat attitude will dissolve into a vision of that high-hat price tag. But, as always, I will forget this lesson, Lord. When I do, remind me again of how fine the line is between fabulous and foolish, outstanding and outlandish, remarkable and ridiculous. When I start to prance and preen, tell me to check the rearview mirror. And thanks, Lord, for such a silly lesson. The tag is gone, but I still can't wipe that snicker off my face!

58 The Trash Man Cometh

If anyone ever asked me to submit a list of my "Ten Most Admired People," do you know who I would have to include? My garbage man!

I realize that Garbage Collector is not exactly one of the most coveted jobs in the world, but my garbage man does his work with pride and efficiency and—believe it or not—with courtesy and cheerfulness. About how many executives can you make that statement?

Now this young man does not look like your average driver of a garbage truck. His blonde good looks would make him eligible to appear in one of the ads you see in magazines or on TV, advertising ski clothing, soft drinks, or any "fun" product. Dressed appropriately, he could mingle at any cocktail party and look like the typical young "comer" on his way up. No one would ever guess that trash is his business.

Usually, he works alone. But some days, he has a helper who lolls along, half-heartedly picking up cans. It's obvious our "hero" does twice the work in half the time. He has his job down to a science, a symphony of movement, timed to make each step count. And yet, he is not so tied to his routine that he can't take time to help.

If any of the neighbors is a bit late putting out the trash and he sees them scurrying toward the curb, he doesn't drive off in a huff to teach them to be on time next week. Instead, he strides up the driveway to take the cans from them and answers apologies with a pleasant "no problem."

You see why his name would have to be on my "admired" list. In today's comfort-oriented society, even those with cushy, well-paid jobs sometimes complain about their "miserable" working conditions. And some employees who are supposed to "serve" the public—in supermarkets, department stores, restaurants—seem insulted if you ask them for any extras. When you call an office for information, you often get surly replies, are transferred from one uninformed employee to another, and then get cut off and have to start all over.

Yet my trash collector continues in his courteous, efficient manner—and even offers a bit of philosophy. One day I had chopped down half a rose bush and had the prickly branches in a pile at the curb. When I heard the rumble of the garbage truck, I dashed out, wearing long sleeves and heavy gloves to protect my arms from the thorns, planning to toss the branches in the truck while Mr. Wonderful emptied the trash cans. But he would have none of it, insisting that he would take care of the branches for me. I cautioned, "Watch out for those thorns—they stick to your clothes." He answered, "Yeah—they're just like love; once they get hold of you, they won't let go."

There are a lot of people who could take lessons from my garbage man. Maybe we all could.

Dear Lord, "work" may be a four-letter word, but it doesn't have to be a dirty one. The next time I have a "dirty" or difficult job to do, remind me to make the best of it instead of whining, procrastinating, and acting like a poor pitiful victim. And the next time I'm down in the dumps, help me to remember the inspiring example of my trash man—so I can get up and get off my can!

59 Whose Label Are You Wearing Today?

Every time I go to pick up my mail at the post office, I feel like a loose woman.

They have all these mailboxes marked for Bulk, Bundles, Express, etc.—and then there's the box for Loose Letters. Now, although I don't write loose letters, my mail is never important enough to be bundled or expressed, so I have no choice but to head for the box labeled "Loose."

Every time I go to the grocery store, I feel like a slow woman. No matter how lean my list is, I never seem to have few enough items to get into the fast lane, so I have no choice but to head for the slow lane.

Every time I go to the gas station, I feel like a self-serving woman. I was taught that it is not nice to be self-serving but what can I do? The only way to save a few pennies is to bypass the full-service pump and head for the one labeled, "Self-Service."

Yes, labels can be limiting and misleading. Some people get "labeled" in childhood and grow up thinking they are not as smart or as attractive as others. Some get a super-critical boss on a first job and spend a career wearing an interior label of inferiority, always on the defensive, always expecting to be corrected or belittled.

For some, a label spells defeat. For others, it becomes a challenge to excel somewhere, somehow—to prove something to the world and to themselves.

But there's one good thing about a label—it can always be changed. Some people change a life-label by moving to a new town and new environment. Some do it by going back to school to learn a new profession or trade or craft. Some make the change by switching on the power of positive thinking.

However, I don't think the post office, grocery store, or gas station will change their labels—so I guess that means I am stuck with being a loose, slow, self-serving woman!

Dear Lord, forgive my foolishness. I know how important it is to ignore labels, to rise above and grow beyond. Lord, I know that some people have given YOU a label too. Some think of you as a harsh taskmaster who must be feared and addressed only in the formal surroundings of a church. Others think of you as all smiles and alleluias and forget about commandments to be obeyed as a way of life. How sad, Lord, to try to limit you when you are limitless, to label you when you are infinite. Thank you, Lord for being a personal friend and at the same time incomprehensible—always beckoning me to delve deeper into your mystery and majesty. And help me to remember, Lord, that the only label I should ever wear is the one that says, "Made by God."

60 On the Sunny Side of the Street

I've been seeing the world through gold-colored glasses. I know, I know. It's supposed to be rose-colored glasses but I never get things quite right.

This all started when a friend went to Florida and brought me some wraparound plastic sunglasses that had two benefits: they cut out all the damaging rays hiding in that glorious summertime brightness AND I could put them on over my reading glasses and see to read in the sunshine.

They were exciting too because they made me look like all I needed was a pilot's cap and a white scarf and I would be ready to take off into the wild blue yonder. The color of the glasses was even a wild blue. And that became a problem.

Those blue glasses made everything in the world look blue. Even on bright, golden days, they made the view blue and somber. All the brilliant red and pink flowers took on a peculiar purple cast. And the sunshine just faded into the blue! I tried to wear them to keep out the rays but I desperately wanted to let in the glow.

Then one day I was at our friendly neighborhood pharmacy. There was a similar pair of glasses, but instead of blue, they were a bright, golden YELLOW. Just to experiment, I tried them on. Hello!—it was a go for the glow! They lit up my life!

When I got home, I took the glasses and a book to the patio. As I glanced around, the flowers seemed brighter, the trees looked greener, and my psyche got perkier. I settled back to enjoy the balmy sunny day. When read-time was up, I took a last look around at the lovely sunniness and then took off the glasses to go inside.

What a shock! Bare-eyed, I realized that the sun was long gone, the sky was totally overcast, and gray clouds were rolling in so fast that by the time I raced into the house, sheets of rain were pelting the patio. I put the glasses back on, and even in the middle of the storm, my garden looked sunny!

Ever since then, I've known just what to do when things look blue. I look at the world through my gold-colored glasses!

Dear Lord, I guess most things in my world can be shaded and colored by my attitude, my way of looking at things. When I have a blue view, even good news can seem bad. But when I have a sunny outlook, I can see that bad news is never totally dark or hopeless. Help me, Lord, to remember that all through history, people have survived and learned from mistakes. Pitfalls have often brought about progress and arguments have resulted in agreements. I know it takes prayer and work to make such things happen but it also takes a BE-attitude. Help me, Lord, to BE hopeful, to BE positive, to BE joyful. Help me to keep my sunny side up!

61 Stop, Look, and Be Surprised

L ast week I decided to hit the road. I would take a simple little trip to visit my sister. In my car. Alone.

It would take no more than six hours of driving along modern, four-lane highways with easy access to gas stations, rest stops, restaurants, and rest rooms. No problem.

No problem until I announced this to my husband and my friends. As soon as they heard I would be driving alone, they began issuing warnings. I should get the car serviced, the oil changed, the tires checked. I should keep my seat belt fastened and put gas in the car. (What a novel idea—gasoline. I would never have thought of THAT!)

My husband cautioned me to keep fresh air in the car by keeping the windows opened a few inches at all times. He didn't want me to drive in a closed car in case something should suddenly go wrong with the exhaust system, causing it to release carbon monoxide in the car, causing me to fall asleep and release my grip on the wheel and run off the road and injure myself or—heaven forbid!—dent the car.

A friend urged me to keep the car doors locked at all times because her son had once been stopped in traffic when a man came running toward him, brandishing a big knife. The man tried to get into the car and would surely have killed her son if all the car doors hadn't been locked.

After considering all this "reassuring" advice, I left on the trip anyway. I put gas in the car and rolled the windows down a bit. And since, most of the way, I was speeding down a highway, I never once saw a knife-wielder running toward my car.

On the way, the trip was uneventful. Coming back was a different matter. I had hardly hit the road when a gully-jumper cloudburst hit. The highway and my windshield were covered with a blinding, gray blanket of rain. Lightning crackled, winds whistled, passing trucks created flash floods, and I was "misted" by raindrops flying through those safely-opened windows. I was not overcome by carbon monoxide fumes—but by terror!

I was afraid to drive fast but I was also afraid to drive slowly for fear someone who couldn't see through the rain would drive OVER me. Before I found a turnoff where I could scurry for cover, I felt like I had been driving 55 mph through a continuous car wash!

After a few rain-stops and rest-stops, I made it safely home. But all the way, I kept thinking that this trip was like the road of life. The things that happen are never the things people warn you about or tell you to guard against. My husband and friends gave me plenty of dire warnings but no one told me to beware dastardly downpours or to pack an Ark in my car trunk!

Dear Lord, people told me marriages are made in heaven but no one mentioned that husbands and wives are responsible for the upkeep and maintenance. Nobody warned me that raising a child can be hazardous to your mental health or that cooking three meals a day creates dirty dishes. Oh well, potholes keep life interesting and I guess surprise is good for the soul. Thank you, Lord, for all the "interesting" surprises you send to get my attention. And help me remember the wise advice another friend gave me: On the road of life, two wrongs do not make a right but three rights DO make a left!

62 It's in the Book!

Covetousness, gluttony, envy, pride, lust, anger, and sloth—I was subjected to and fell under the spell of all seven deadly sins this week. I went to a Book Fair!

Under a gigantic tent, rows and rows of tables held thousands of books. Since I love books, I COVETED them all. As I stepped on some toes and elbowed my way through the crowd, I GLUT-TONOUSLY grabbed books of every shape and size—some almost-new, some well-thumbed and dog-eared, some serious, some funny. And I was filled with PRIDE at all the bargains I had been shrewd enough to spot.

Even though my shopping bag was stuffed and dragging the floor, I unashamedly peeked over the shoulders of strangers to see the titles of the books they were clutching, ENVYING the treasures they had beat me out of.

Then, as I approached the "rare" book section, I LUSTED after the exotic, expensive books displayed there, knowing I couldn't afford any of them. And as I glanced at my watch, I gave in to ANGER, because I was running out of time and money and I didn't want to leave.

There was only one of the seven deadly sins left. But of course, soon after I got home, SLOTH took over as I let the housework go and pored over my Book Fair fare. I lovingly paged through the humor books, cookbooks, mysteries, and miscellaneous. Then I noted a great quote in one of the really old books. It was from an 1870 news item: "A waspishly small waist no longer excites admiration—the spirituelle figures are not considered stylish nowadays; deep, healthy shoulders and plump, round waists of twenty-two and twenty-three inches are now the fashion." TWENTY-TWO inches? Our Thanksgiving turkey had a waist plumper than that!

Another quote concerned dining etiquette of 1875: "It is well to carry in your pocket a small pincushion, and, having folded your napkin, to pin it at the belt." And then there was a page of advertising which offered a sale on lady's hairpieces—"fine braids, waterfalls, puffs, and frizzled curls."

All of that sounds pretty funny today but those ideas just might be helpful. With a napkin pinned at a twenty-two-inch waist, a pincushion in your pocket, and a waterfall on your head, you'd be much too restrained to commit any of those seven deadly sins!

Dear Lord, thank you for today. It's fun to read about once-upon-a-time but I wouldn't want to live there. I realized that when I looked at the title of another of my bargain books—"Dream House: It could be the house you're living in now." The book offered home remodeling ideas but it made me think about how often I pine and whine about wanting a dream house, a dream job, a dream family—when I might already have them.

Maybe instead of painting over problems, I need to look at them more honestly. Maybe I need to rearrange an attitude, tear down a wall of resentment, or put in a new window of understanding. Maybe with some remodeling work and some prayer, the "dream life" I crave could be my own!

63 Games People Play

Well, it happened again. This morning, I had a case of the sniffles. So I looked pitiful and asked my husband to make the coffee.

He said, "Sure! Where's the coffee?"

I said, "In the kitchen cupboard where it always is."

He said, "Which kitchen cupboard?"

I said, "The one next to the refrigerator."

He said, "Which shelf is it on in the cupboard?"

I said, "On the bottom one, next to the cereal."

He said, "What color is the label on the can so I can recognize it?"

I said, "Never mind."

The same thing happens when I ask him to pick up something at a store for me. He says, "Which street is the store on? Which SIDE of the street is it on? Where do I park? Once I get in the store, which aisle do I look in? Where is the checkout counter? Should I pay with cash, a check, or charge card?"

And I say, "Never mind."

As the old saying goes, "It pays to be ignorant." And, as another saying should go, "It takes a smart man to be able to PLAY ignorant only when he knows it will PAY to be ignorant."

It wouldn't be so bad if my husband hadn't passed on his knowledge of the game to the next generation so that now my son can also keep up the questioning until his mother sighs and replies, "Never mind."

Of course, those two are not as smart as they think. I know even more than they do about playing to win so I see to it that neither father nor son can get away with too much for too long. I let them have their chance and then I take mine. But I am also old enough to have learned that if you play to win ALL the time, you are the one who ends up the loser.

Dear Lord, our games are just silly ones. We never try to one-up each other when the stakes are important. But today, the Family Game is sometimes very serious and no fun any more. The media tries to tell us that the rules have changed and some people believe that. The children end up running the store instead of the parents, nice guys DO finish last, and everyone is the loser.

Help us, Lord. Help us to remember that the commandments are still "relevant" and there is no new eleventh commandment that says it's OK to "do your own thing." Help us, Lord, to know when it is time to discuss and dialogue and when it is time to stand up and say what we believe. And thank you, Lord, for paying attention to my chatter. I do sometimes wonder if you keep listening but I know deep down that you are there. That's why I never give up and say to you, "Never mind." And that's why I know you will never give up and say to me, "Never mind."

64 Why Is There Mildew in My Milieu?

When I look up the word "mildew" in my dictionary, it describes it as a "whitish growth produced by fungi." If only that were true at my house. I have white bathroom tile so the mildew would blend right in. Of course, nothing else "blends in" in my milieu—so why should the mildew?

Unfortunately, the stuff in my shower is more blackish than whitish. And after further research (done when I SHOULD have been scrubbing the shower), I have discovered that my family has gifted me with "chiaroscuro." This is the name which my *Reverse Dictionary* gives to "black and white, light and shadow." That's my shower all right!

No matter how often I remove that darling fungi, the next time I turn on the light, there it is lurking in the shadows—black on white.

Oh well, I guess that's a sign that at least SOMETHING is growing in our house. I wish I was growing taller or smarter or more patient. I wish my budget was growing fatter instead of leaner. I wish my lawn was growing greener instead of weedier. So maybe I should be grateful for this FIRST sign of growth!

But, if I have to have fungi growing in our house, why couldn't it be those elusive truffles that cost a fortune? Why do I have to have plain, ordinary mildew in our milieu?

* * * * * *

Dear Lord, maybe it's good that my mildew is black instead of white. Then, at least, I can spot the "darkness" and scrub it out before it grows too far. If only I could do that with all the other growing darkness in today's world. My octogenarian friend, Mary, used to recite a poem to me about that, Lord. I don't remember the exact words but I'll never forget the message. It warned, "When first you meet evil, you are repelled and disgusted. The next time you meet, you've seen it before so you tolerate it. Soon you accept it and finally welcome it."

Help me, Lord, to realize how dangerous today's snickering acceptance can be. Keep me alert to the little specks before they grow into big black specters. Maybe then, Lord, I can do a better job of getting rid of all this dark mildew in my milieu!

65 Globe-Trotting in My Own Home Town

I took a trip around the world one day this week and I didn't even need a supersonic jet—just my old, beat-up car.

It started simply enough when I picked up a friend to go out for lunch. We left our modern, typical subdivision and drove just a few miles across town to lunch leisurely in the garden of a charming old castle-like restaurant. We felt as though we were hundreds of miles from home in some elegant European capital.

After lunch, we decided to skip the highway and to go home by way of a meandering side-street route. We passed through a section of town that seemed "foreign" to us. Unlike the sameness of our neighborhood, this cozy old area has all kinds of architecture—a square, no-nonsense brick house might sit next to a gabled white frame one, a turreted stone "fortress," or a home decorated with the lacework of a black wrought iron balcony and fence. There are red-tiled roofs, long porches, brick walks, and flowers in window boxes.

Adjoining that area is one full of little "mom and pop" stores—a bakery, a small grocery, a "variety" store, an antique shop, a barbershop. People stroll along the street "window shopping" and stopping to visit with friends. And there are lots of mommies pushing baby carriages.

Later that afternoon, I had errands to run in still another part of town and this took me through a very poor section that was not cheerfully charming. Yet there too were touches of joy—tiny, pocket-sized flowerbeds, bikes on porches, and pretty curtains in some windows.

Adjoining that area was a manufacturing section where everything was strictly business—factories, warehouses, loading docks, trucks. There were few bits of architectural interest but the area was alive with the busy wheels of industry.

My around-the-world trip in a day reminded me of something I read about the nineteenth century. Architects then believed that buildings could influence behavior. They felt that medieval towns had been beautiful and moral, whereas utilitarian, industrial towns were grim and hateful. In the hope that the "imagery" of architecture could help solve social problems of that day, they put up Gothic structures to inspire people with memories of a chivalrous past and "classical" buildings as a reminder of the art and culture of ancient Greece and Rome. The eclectic "fruit salad" of Victorian architecture was not frivolous; it was the result of sober-minded people trying to make their world better.

So what about our architecture today? Do those cold glass-and-chrome buildings contribute to a cold, calculated approach to business? Do smug, closed-in homes that keep us apart from neighbors' joys and sorrows make it easy to focus on "me-first, me-only"? Hmmm... I wonder.

*．＊．＊．＊．＊

Dear Lord, thank you for the diversity of buildings and of people. Help me to appreciate that and to recognize the beauty of all. And, Lord, help me to be a builder too. Help me to make the "architecture" of my home and my world more inspiring, more gracious, more blessed. Thank you, Lord, for my trip around the world today. It was very educational!

66 Apple-Bobbing

If an apple a day keeps the doctor away, I could have dropped my health insurance this year.

When we moved into this house, a scraggly little apple tree was growing out by the patio and a tree "expert" told me I might as well chop it down unless I just wanted shade because it would never have an apple on it. For some unknown reason, the former owners of the house had sawed off the top of the main trunk of the tree and all the branches were "suckers" growing out of the sides in an unmannerly fashion.

Well, I did want shade and besides, I liked the little suckers! So I did not chop down the apple tree. It stayed by our patio and quietly grew and cast a bit more shade each year. Then, one springtime, it rewarded us for our friendship. We looked out the window one morning and saw a picture-perfect tree totally covered with a froth of fluffy, white apple blossoms. We reveled in the beauty while it lasted and wondered if the blossoms would turn into apples. In the fall, there were three little apples on the tree.

Since then, each springtime the tree has put on a show of incredible beauty and each fall, it has produced a few inedible apples. But this year was different.

Another expert came by and said we better get all our trees sprayed to protect them against the effects of this year's drought and the dread diseases sure to follow. So the apple tree got sprayed along with the others. And this was just what it had been waiting for. Suddenly, we had a bushel and a peck of apples—plus a lesson to be learned.

As I picked and peeled those apples, I began to think of how some people are like our apple tree. Even though they've been "stunted," sawed off by lack of education, money or opportunity, they've still managed to flourish and give others whatever gifts they could muster—comforting shade, blossoming beauty, fruits of the Spirit.

They put to shame others who have been given so much, and return so little.

Dear Lord, thank you for the apple tree and all the apple pies we've been enjoying. I was surprised to find when I cut into some apples that looked as pretty as a picture on the outside; inside, they were rotten to the core. Others that looked kind of scruffy on the outside were perfect on the inside and absolutely delicious. Help me to remember that, Lord, when I watch TV and see so much that is glittery and beautiful and I start to hunger and yearn for what I don't have and forget to be glad for what I do have. And on those days, Lord, when I'm struggling on rocky ground and feel like a "sucker," remind me that, like the apple tree, I can still bloom where I was planted.

67 Family Secrets

What are the "secrets of the universe"? Ask any mother and she can tell you a few! I can tell you about Inflection/Reflection Reaction (IRR), Telephone Telepathy, and many others.

You probably already know about IRR. That's when an out-of-sight kid suddenly lets out a scream loud enough to turn the air purple. His mother never even flinches. She just goes right on cleaning the oven, inventing a cure for the common jelly stain, or stitching up a crocodile costume for the school play. That's because the kid's INFLECTION is wrong.

Another time that same kid can let out a similar scream and the mother will drop everything mid-air to dash frantically to the scene of the scream—and to the rescue!

Evidently a mother's reaction depends on something like that high-pitched whistle that can be heard only by dogs. The emergency child-sound can be heard only by mothers, not by innocent bystanders. Our "trained" ears reflect on the inflection and instantly detect the difference between a momentary frustration or irritation and a genuine RED ALERT.

Now Telephone Telepathy is another mystery. Any mother will tell you that the minute she gets on the telephone, a child will suddenly appear at her elbow. The house can be deserted when she picks up the phone but somehow, within seconds, a child will appear from nowhere to tug at Mommy and whine loudly for immediate attention.

That child could have been next door or down the block or in a soundproof room busily drawing a detailed picture of a nuclear bomb for show-and-tell. It doesn't matter. The minute Mommy gets on the phone and starts to explain to the electric compan that their computer must have made a mistake because a family of four could not possibly use enough electricity in one month to get a bill for three million dollars—that's the minute the child's Telephone Telepathy will tell him or her to hurry to Mommy's side for a whine time.

But I have just now discovered a lesser-known secret of the universe. It seems that even children who no longer live at home know exactly the WRONG minute to communicate with a parent.

Friends tell me that the minute they are dashing out the door to go to an important meeting, party, or dentist appointment, the phone will ring. It will be a married daughter or a college-age son who has suddenly decided it is time for a nice friendly chat with the folks. They may not have heard from that child for weeks and they may be hungry for news and conversation but the ONLY time an "away" child will be in the mood to talk is at the moment Mom or Dad is hurrying out the door—and running late.

It seems that children never outgrow Telephone Telepathy.

₊₊*₊*₊*

Dear Lord, thank you for telephones and children who call. It must have been awful for the pioneers whose children left in covered wagons and could only communicate with them via pony express. But, Lord, it does seem that when you built in that telepathy you could have used a little better timing device!

68 What's in a Word?

I was spending my valuable time working a crossword puzzle today—telling myself it would improve my IQ and my word power, and my knowledge of the world in general. Actually, it was just an excuse to rest my feet a few minutes and indulge in some word play.

When I got stuck on a difficult clue, I began to think about how the English language is a lot like a child—sometimes delightful, sometimes confusing, and sometimes downright maddening. Some words have such built-in beauty, they can make you feel good just to hear the lilt in them. Others have so many different meanings and interpretations that you must be very careful how you handle them. Like a child, the English language can charm you—or it can drive you up the wall, make you nutty, or cause you to go bananas!

See what I mean? We have such silly English expressions. "Drive you up the wall"? How? In a stretch-limo? With a fire hose? With the help of a mountain climber attached to a strong rope?

And how does someone make you "nutty"? Spread you with peanut butter? Hoist you into a walnut tree?

"Go bananas"—what's that mean? Turn yellow? Get a thick skin? Start to hang around with a bunch?

One of the funniest parts of the English language involves the naming of groups of things. I can understand a "swarm of bees" or a "flock of geese" but who came up with the idea of a school of fish, a pride of lions, a host of angels?

Abandoning my puzzle, I began to waste time by putting together some groupings of my own. How about a gaggle of gossips or a wiggle of women, a passel of prophets or a hassle of husbands, a clatter of children or a mutter of mothers?

Well, this just shows how easy it is for minds to meander and thoughts to travel—and still get nowhere fast.

Dear Lord, word play can be fun but it has reminded me that I should be much more careful. You know how quickly and easily words roll off my tongue—but sometimes they land with a thud on the ears and hearts of those who hear them. Help me, Lord, to think before I speak. And when I can't manage that, help me to think AFTER I speak. Help me to be quick to find some calming, balming words to try to undo the damage I have done and make it all better again. Lord, when we're babies, you let us learn how to talk in only two years—but it takes some of us a lifetime to learn when NOT TO talk. Help me to learn that, Lord, before I get much older. Help me to break the habit so I can enjoy a healthier diet. I'm so tired of always having to eat my own words.

69 Zoo's Who?

I ate an elephant this morning. Then I chewed a camel, bit a bear, and munched a monkey. Later, I just might chomp a cougar, chew a kangaroo, or steal a seal. Yep, I have rediscovered those childhood yumyums—animal crackers!

How could I resist them? They were on sale. And I'll buy almost anything that's on sale. I'm especially glad I did this time. With bulls and bears and the big bad wolf lurking around every corner today, it's very reassuring to meet a "sweet" ferocious animal!

I had forgotten what fun it is to have a little box with a string handle. Wouldn't it be great if we could get a handle on all our fears by carrying them around in a little box with a handle—and then eat them up instead of letting them eat on us!

Of course, there are those who might think that eating animal crackers indicates I am entering my second childhood and making a monkey out of myself. But maybe that's not too bad.

Monkeys are friendly and funny. They eat a healthy diet—with lots of fruit. They are fast learners and fast movers. They are good entertainers and often make people laugh and feel happy. Children like them.

So maybe it's OK to make a monkey out of yourself once in a while!

* * * * *

Dear Lord, it's no wonder children love animal crackers. We read them fairy tales about the spider who frightened Miss Muffet, the wolf who ate a grandmother, and the blackbird who bit off the maid-hanging-out-clothes' nose! No wonder they want to bite back. No wonder I do too. It's a scary world out there, Lord. Sometimes I too feel like a child, afraid of the dark and the monster lurking under the bed waiting to eat my toes. But then, Lord, I remember that you are with me always so the only thing I have to fear is fear itself! In fact, I feel so brave right now, Lord, that I think I will go on a kitchen safari and have a lion for lunch!

70 Thoughts for Your Daze

I've been doing it again. Taking the easy way out. Opting for the shortcut. Looking for quick answers.

Yep, instead of reading deep theological books and immersing myself in meditation, I've been getting my inspiration by reading T-shirt and bumper sticker slogans. naughty.

Since I have been known to try many new diets, I naturally noticed this T-shirt wisecrack: "The body is fueled by the four basic food groups: Chocolate Candy, Chocolate Brownies, Chocolate Ice Cream, and Diet Cola." Unfortunately, that IS my kind of fuel.

But then there was the shirt that boasted, "Veni, Vidi, Vegi: I came, I saw, I had a salad." And the most inspirational of all bragged, "Bless me, Lord, for I have thinned."

Switching from food to friendship, I love the message, "A true friend remembers your birthday—but not which one it is."

How fortunate I am to have so many kind and forgetful friends! Which brings me to another favorite, "Too much of a good thing can be wonderful."

And I like this one too: "Please, Lord, let me PROVE to you that winning a magazine sweepstakes won't spoil me."

Well, I guess I'm already spoiled. I have all those great friends and the opportunity to choose between salad and chocolate— even if I DO too often make the wrong choice. And I also have lots of excitement in my life. I was reminded of that when I saw the T-shirt which read, "Marriages are made in heaven, but so are thunder and lightning."

* * * * * * *

Dear Lord, forgive my shallowness. Help me to NOT settle for cute sayings or slogans. Help me to keep studying, seeking, and yearning for truth—wherever I find it.

Today I saw a greeting card with this message: "God uses broken things. Broken soil produces a good crop, broken clouds shower down refreshing rain, broken grain makes hearty loaves of bread, and bread broken with family and friends turns into a communion of love and sharing." Lord, what a reassuring and hopeful thought for a person who has a broken hairdryer, a broken vacuum cleaner, and many broken resolutions. I may live with brokenness but I know you will use that to make me whole. And I also know that no matter how many times I break my resolutions, YOU will never break your promises. I thank you, Lord. I need you, Lord. I love you, Lord. With you by my side, life is so much fun!

Other titles by Bernadette McCarver Snyder include:

That's Life!

Heavenly Hash

The Fun Facts Dictionary

150 Fun Facts Found in the Bible...for Kids of All Ages

*Painting Rainbows with Broken Crayons: 101 Prayers
for Teachers, Parents, and other Caretakers*

Graham Crackers, Galoshes, and God

Every Woman's Book of Cope and Hope